CSWE's Core Competencies and Practice Behavior Examples in this Text

Competency	Chapter
Professional Identity	
Practice Behavior Examples...	
Serve as representatives of the profession, its mission, and its core values	9, 10, 11, 13
Know the profession's history	
Commit themselves to the profession's enhancement and to their own professional conduct and growth	1
Advocate for client access to the services of social work	1, 6, 7, 8, 9, 10, 11, 12, 13
Practice personal reflection and self-correction to assure continual professional development	1, 6, 7
Attend to professional roles and boundaries	1, 8, 9, 10, 11
Demonstrate professional demeanor in behavior, appearance, and communication	4, 6, 7
Engage in career-long learning	
Use supervision and consultation	1, 6, 7, 9, 10, 11
Gerontology Practice Behavior Examples...	
Assess and address values and biases regarding aging	1, 5, 6, 7, 8, 9, 10, 11, 12, 13
Understand the perspective and values of social work in relation to working effectively with other disciplines in geriatric interdisciplinary practice	1, 5, 6, 7, 8, 9, 10, 11, 12, 13
Ethical Practice	
Practice Behavior Examples...	
Obligation to conduct themselves ethically and engage in ethical decision-making	1, 11
Know about the value base of the profession, its ethical standards, and relevant law	1, 5, 8, 9, 10, 11, 12
Recognize and manage personal values in a way that allows professional values to guide practice	1, 5, 6, 7, 9, 11, 12
Make ethical decisions by applying standards of the National Association of Social Workers Code of Ethics and, as applicable, of the International Federation of Social Workers/International Association of Schools of Social Work Ethics in Social Work, Statement of Principles	1, 5, 11
Tolerate ambiguity in resolving ethical conflicts	1, 5, 10, 11
Apply strategies of ethical reasoning to arrive at principled decisions	6, 7, 8, 9, 11
Gerontology Practice Behavior Examples...	
Apply ethical principles to decisions on behalf of all older clients with special attention to those who have limited decisional capacity	3, 5, 6, 7, 9, 10, 11, 12
Assess "self in relation" to motivate themselves and others toward mutual, meaningful achievement of a focused goal or committed standard of practice	1, 3, 5, 6, 7, 8, 9, 10, 11, 12

Adapted with the permission of Council on Social Work Education

CSWE's Core Competencies and Practice Behavior Examples in this Text

Competency	Chapter
Critical Thinking	
Practice Behavior Examples...	
Know about the principles of logic, scientific inquiry, and reasoned discernment	2, 5, 6, 7, 12
Use critical thinking augmented by creativity and curiosity	3, 5, 6, 7, 10, 11, 12
Requires the synthesis and communication of relevant information	2, 4, 6, 7, 9
Distinguish, appraise, and integrate multiple sources of knowledge, including research-based knowledge, and practice wisdom	1, 3, 5, 8, 9, 11, 12
Analyze models of assessment, prevention, intervention, and evaluation	2, 4, 5, 6, 7, 8, 10
Demonstrate effective oral and written communication in working with individuals, families, groups, organizations, communities, and colleagues	4
Gerontology Practice Behavior Examples...	
Relate concepts and theories of aging to social work practice (e.g., cohorts, normal aging, and life course perspective)	1, 2, 3, 5, 6, 7, 8, 9, 11
Communicate to public audiences and policy makers through multiple media, including writing synthesis reports and legislative statements and orally presenting the mission and outcomes of the services of an organization or for diverse client groups	13
Diversity in Practice	
Practice Behavior Examples...	
Understand how diversity characterizes and shapes the human experience and is critical to the formation of identity	1, 2, 3, 4, 8, 9, 10, 11
Understand the dimensions of diversity as the intersectionality of multiple factors including age, class, color, culture, disability, ethnicity, gender, gender identity and expression, immigration status, political ideology, race, religion, sex, and sexual orientation	1, 3, 4, 5, 8, 9, 10, 11, 12
Appreciate that, as a consequence of difference, a person's life experiences may include oppression, poverty, marginalization, and alienation as well as privilege, power, and acclaim	1, 5, 13
Recognize the extent to which a culture's structures and values may oppress, marginalize, alienate, or create or enhance privilege and power	9, 13
Gain sufficient self-awareness to eliminate the influence of personal biases and values in working with diverse groups	1, 9
Recognize and communicate their understanding of the importance of difference in shaping life experiences	2, 4, 5, 6, 7, 8, 9, 10, 13
View themselves as learners and engage those with whom they work as informants	2, 6, 9, 11
Gerontology Practice Behavior Examples...	
Respect diversity among older adult clients, families, and professionals (e.g., class, race, ethnicity, gender, and sexual orientation)	1, 2, 3, 4, 5, 6, 7, 8, 9, 10, 11, 12
Address the cultural, spiritual, and ethnic values and beliefs of older adults and families.	1, 3, 4, 5, 6, 7, 8, 9, 10, 11, 12, 13

Competency	Chapter
Human Rights & Justice	
Practice Behavior Examples...	
Understand that each person, regardless of position in society, has basic human rights, such as freedom, safety, privacy, an adequate standard of living, health care, and education	1, 9, 11, 13
Recognize the global interconnections of oppression and are knowledgeable about theories of justice and strategies to promote human and civil rights	1, 13
Incorporates social justice practices in organizations, institutions, and society to ensure that these basic human rights are distributed equitably and without prejudice	11, 13
Understand the forms and mechanisms of oppression and discrimination	1
Advocate for human rights and social and economic justice	9
Engage in practices that advance social and economic justice	1, 9
Gerontology Practice Behavior Examples...	
Respect and promote older adult clients' right to dignity and self-determination	1, 4, 5, 6, 9, 10, 11, 12
Assess and address any negative impacts of social and health care policies on practice with historically disadvantaged populations	1, 4, 5, 6, 7, 9, 10, 11, 12, 13
Research Based Practice	
Practice Behavior Examples...	
Use practice experience to inform research, employ evidence-based interventions, evaluate their own practice, and use research findings to improve practice, policy, and social service delivery	2, 3, 5, 6, 7, 8, 9
Comprehend quantitative and qualitative research and understand scientific and ethical approaches to building knowledge	2, 8
Use practice experience to inform scientific inquiry	4, 5, 6, 7, 8
Use research evidence to inform practice	2, 4, 5, 6, 7, 8
Gerontology Practice Behavior Examples...	
Evaluate the effectiveness of practice and programs in achieving intended outcomes for older adults	5, 6, 7, 8, 11, 12, 13
Promote the use of research (including evidence-based practice) to evaluate and enhance the effectiveness of social work practice and aging related services	5, 6, 7, 8, 10, 11, 12, 13
Human Behavior	
Practice Behavior Examples...	
Know about human behavior across the life course; the range of social systems in which people live; and the ways social systems promote or deter people in maintaining or achieving health and well-being	1, 2, 3, 4, 5, 6, 7, 9, 10, 11, 12, 13
Apply theories and knowledge from the liberal arts to understand biological, social, cultural, psychological, and spiritual development	2, 3, 4, 5, 6, 7, 10
Utilize conceptual frameworks to guide the processes of assessment, intervention, and evaluation	4, 5, 6, 7, 8
Critique and apply knowledge to understand person and environment.	2, 3, 4, 5, 6, 7, 8, 9, 10, 11, 12

CSWE's Core Competencies and Practice Behavior Examples in this Text

Competency	Chapter
Gerontology Practice Behavior Examples...	
Relate social work perspectives and related theories to practice with older adults	2, 3, 4, 5, 6, 7, 8, 9, 10, 11, 12
Identify issues related to losses, changes, and transitions over their life cycle in designing interventions	1, 3, 4, 5, 6, 7, 8, 9, 10, 11, 12
Policy Practice	
Practice Behavior Examples...	
Understand that policy affects service delivery and they actively engage in policy practice	
Know the history and current structures of social policies and services; the role of policy in service delivery; and the role of practice in policy development	9, 11, 13
Analyze, formulate, and advocate for policies that advance social well-being	9, 13
Collaborate with colleagues and clients for effective policy action	
Gerontology Practice Behavior Examples...	
Adapt organizational policies, procedures, and resources to facilitate the provision of services to diverse older adults and their family caregivers	1, 11, 12, 13
Manage individual (personal) and multi-stakeholder (interpersonal) processes at the community, interagency, and intra-agency levels to inspire and leverage power and resources to optimize services for older adults	9, 11, 12, 13
Practice Contexts	
Practice Behavior Examples...	
Keep informed, resourceful, and proactive in responding to evolving organizational, community, and societal contexts at all levels of practice	1, 9, 11, 12, 13
Recognize that the context of practice is dynamic, and use knowledge and skill to respond proactively	2, 11, 12, 13
Continuously discover, appraise, and attend to changing locales, populations, scientific and technological developments, and emerging societal trends to provide relevant services	1, 11, 12, 13
Provide leadership in promoting sustainable changes in service delivery and practice to improve the quality of social services	12, 13
Gerontology Practice Behavior Examples...	
Create a shared organizational mission, vision, values, and policies responding to ever-changing service systems to promote coordinated optimal services for older persons	1, 13
Advocate and organize with service providers, community organizations, policy makers, and the public to meet the needs of a growing aging population	1, 9, 11, 13
Engage, Assess Intervene, Evaluate	
Practice Behavior Examples...	
Identify, analyze, and implement evidence-based interventions designed to achieve client goals	6, 7, 8, 9, 10
Use research and technological advances	2, 5, 6, 7, 8, 9, 11
Evaluate program outcomes and practice effectiveness	

Competency	Chapter
Develop, analyze, advocate, and provide leadership for policies and services	13
Promote social and economic justice	4, 5, 6, 7, 8, 9, 11
A) ENGAGEMENT	
Substantively and effectively prepare for action with individuals, families, groups, organizations, and communities	
Use empathy and other interpersonal skills	4, 5, 6, 7, 8, 9, 11
Develop a mutually agreed- n focus of work and desired outcomes	6, 7, 8, 9, 10, 11
Gerontology Practice Behavior Examples...	
Establish rapport and maintain effective working relationships with older adults and family members	4, 5, 6, 7, 8, 9, 11, 12
B) ASSESSMENT	2, 3, 4, 5, 6, 7, 8, 9, 10, 11
Collect, organize, and interpret client data	
Assess client strengths and limitations	2, 3, 4, 5, 6, 7, 8, 9, 10, 11, 12
Develop mutually agreed-on intervention goals and objectives	4, 6, 7, 8, 9, 10
Select appropriate intervention strategies	4, 6, 7, 8, 9, 10, 11, 12
Gerontology Practice Behavior Examples...	
Conduct a comprehensive geriatric assessment (biopsychosocial evaluation)	4, 5, 9
Administer and interpret standardized assessment and diagnostic tools that are appropriate for use with older adults (e.g., depression scale, Mini-Mental Status Exam)	4, 5, 10, 11, 12
C) INTERVENTION	
Initiate actions to achieve organizational goals	
Implement prevention interventions that enhance client capacities	5, 6, 7, 8, 10, 11, 12
Help clients resolve problems	5, 6, 7, 10, 11, 12, 13
Negotiate, mediate, and advocate for clients	8, 9, 13
Facilitate transitions and endings	7, 8, 9, 11, 12, 13
Gerontology Practice Behavior Examples...	
Use group interventions with older adults and their families (e.g., bereavement groups, reminiscence groups)	6, 7, 8, 10, 11, 12
Provide social work case management to link elders and their families to resources and services	4, 6, 7, 8, 9, 10, 11, 12, 13
D) EVALUATION	
Critically analyze, monitor, and evaluate interventions	6, 7, 8, 9, 12
Gerontology Practice Behavior Examples...	
Develop clear, timely, and appropriate service plans with measurable objectives for older adults	4, 5, 6, 7, 8, 9, 10, 11, 12
Reevaluate and adjust service plans for older adults on a continuing basis	5, 6, 7, 8, 9, 10, 11, 12

Competency	Chapter
Develop, analyze, advocate, and provide leadership for policies and services	13
Promote social and economic justice	4, 5, 6, 7, 8, 9, 11
A) ENGAGEMENT	
Substantively and effectively prepare for action with individuals, families, groups, organizations, and communities	
Use empathy and other interpersonal skills	4, 5, 6, 7, 8, 9, 11
Develop a mutually agreed-on focus of work and desired outcomes	6, 7, 8, 9, 10, 11
Gerontology Practice Behavior Examples.	
Establish rapport and maintain effective working relationships with older adults and family members	4, 5, 6, 7, 8, 9, 11, 12
B) ASSESSMENT	2, 3, 4, 5, 6, 7, 8, 9, 10, 11
Collect, organize, and interpret client data.	
Assess client strengths and limitations	2, 3, 4, 5, 6, 7, 8, 9, 10, 11, 12
Develop mutually agreed-on intervention goals and objectives.	4, 6, 7, 8, 9, 10
Select appropriate intervention strategies.	4, 6, 7, 8, 9, 10, 11, 12
Gerontology Practice Behavior Examples.	
Conduct a comprehensive general assessment (biopsychosocial evaluation)	4, 5, 9
Administer and interpret standardized assessment and diagnostic tools that are appropriate for use with older adults (e.g., depression scale, Mini-Mental Status Exam)	4, 5, 10, 11, 12
C) INTERVENTION	
Initiate actions to achieve organizational goals.	
Implement prevention interventions that enhance client capacities	5, 6, 7, 8, 10, 11, 12
Help clients resolve problems	5, 6, 7, 10, 11, 12, 13
Negotiate, mediate, and advocate for clients	5, 8, 13
Facilitate transitions and endings	7, 8, 9, 11, 12, 13
Gerontology Practice Behavior Examples.	
Use group interventions with older adults and their families (e.g., bereavement groups, reminiscence groups)	6, 7, 8, 10, 11, 13
Provide social work case management to link elders and their families to resources and services	4, 6, 7, 8, 9, 10, 11, 12, 13
D) EVALUATION	
Critically analyze, monitor, and evaluate interventions	6, 7, 8, 9, 12
Gerontology Practice Behavior Examples.	
Develop clear, timely, and appropriate service plans with measurable objectives for older adults	4, 5, 6, 7, 8, 9, 10, 11, 12
Reevaluate and adjust service plans for older adults on a continuing basis	5, 6, 7, 8, 9, 10, 11, 12

Social Work with Older Adults

A Biopsychosocial Approach to Assessment and Intervention

Kathleen McInnis-Dittrich

Boston College

PEARSON

Boston   Columbus   Indianapolis   New York   San Francisco   Upper Saddle River
Amsterdam   Cape Town   Dubai   London   Madrid   Milan   Munich   Paris   Montréal   Toronto
Delhi   Mexico City   São Paulo   Sydney   Hong Kong   Seoul   Singapore   Taipei   Tokyo

In memory of my father,
William R. McInnis

Editorial Director: Craig Campanella
Editor in Chief: Ashley Dodge
Editorial Product Manager: Carly Czech
Editorial Assistant: Nicole Suddeth
Vice President/Director of Marketing: Brandy Dawson
Executive Marketing Manager: Kelly May
Marketing Coordinator: Courtney Stewart
Senior Media Editor: Paul DeLuca
Editorial Production and Composition Service: PreMediaGlobal
Production Project Manager: Liz Napolitano
Manager, Central Design: Jayne Conte
Interior Design: Joyce Weston Design
Cover Designer: Karen Noferi
Cover Image: © James Thew/Fotolia
Printer/Binder/Cover Printer: R.R. Donnelley/Harrisonburg
Text Font: 10/12 Minion Pro

Credits and acknowledgments borrowed from other sources and reproduced, with permission, in this textbook appear on the appropriate page within text.

Library of Congress Cataloging-in-Publication Data

McInnis-Dittrich, Kathleen
  Social work with older adults: a biopsychosocial approach to assessment and intervention/Kathleen McInnis-Dittrich.—4th ed.
    p. cm.
  Includes bibliographical references and index.
  ISBN-13: 978-0-205-09672-5
  ISBN-10: 0-205-09672-7
1. Social work with older people—United States. 2. Older people—Services for—United States.
3. Aging—United States. I. Title.
  HV1461.M384 2014
  362.60973—dc23
                                                                            2012037969

10 9 8 7 6

ISBN-10:   0-205-09672-7
ISBN-13: 978-0-205-09672-5

Contents

8. Substance Abuse and Suicide Prevention in Older Adults   202

12. Working with Older Adults' Support Systems: Spouses, Partners, Families, and Caregivers 315

Preface

There is little doubt that social work with older adults is one of the hottest areas of social work practice today. As the baby boomer generation moves from middle age to old age, the sheer size of this population and its birth cohort's experience of promoting rapid social change will force the profession to develop new and innovative approaches to practice. No social institution has remained unchanged as this population has moved through the life cycle. Education, health care, the workplace, and family life have all been transformed by the needs and interests of this generation. Likewise, social workers and other helping professionals can expect this group to forge new models of what constitutes "successful aging." This is a very exciting time to be studying gerontological social work!

The generous support of the John A. Hartford Foundation through the Geriatric Education Enrichment Project has been instrumental in encouraging and enabling social work programs throughout the United States to infuse content on aging into all parts of the curriculum. The Hartford Partnership Program for Aging Education (HPPAE) in recent years has supported the effort of field education programs to expose students to a wider variety of field experiences through its focus on the rotational model of field experiences. Rather than treat aging as a separate and often invisible part of social work education, these projects have offered numerous resources for incorporating relevant aging content in human behavior and the social environment, social welfare policy, research, as well as social work practice and field education. On behalf of the Boston College Graduate School of Social Work, one of the recipients of a Geriatric Education Enrichment and HPPAE grants, I thank the foundation for including social work among those professions recognized as having a vital role in improving the quality of service to older adults.

Over the years, I have been fortunate to have worked with an extraordinary group of older adults in both personal and professional contexts. My maternal grandmother presented such a vivacious and delightful picture of the joys of being an older adult that it was not until much later in my life that I truly realized that aging has its challenges as well as its joys. She had such a positive, enthusiastic attitude about life, even in the face of much personal sorrow, that I learned to cherish the idea of growing older long before I saw any reason to fear it. In my professional life, I have seen the remarkable personal strength of older adults—from older adults living in the Central City Housing Project in New Orleans to the older adults living in the Appalachian Mountains in Kentucky to older adults living on the American Indian reservations of Wisconsin. The fortitude that helped these older adults survive the bleakest poverty and greatest social oppression has helped them move through old age as true survivors. I have learned over a cup of coffee as much about aging from these older adults—with whom I have shared the deep pain of the loss of a loved one to Alzheimer's disease, the joys of grandparenthood, or the challenges of learning to balance a checkbook for the first time—as I have learned from any professional literature.

This book presents a comprehensive overview of the field of gerontological social work, from the basics of the biopsychosocial changes associated with the aging process through the assessment of strengths and challenges to the design and execution of problem-solving interventions. *Social Work with Older Adults* is written for both undergraduate and graduate students in courses addressing social work practice with older adults, focusing on interventions with individual older adults, older adults' support systems, and groups of older adults. It is intended to cover topics as basic as encouraging older adults to exercise to those as complex as the process of differential assessment and diagnosis of depression, dementia, or delirium. The topics covered throughout the book are relevant to practitioners working in social service agencies, nursing homes, congregate and assisted-living centers, and adult day health.

Unlike many other texts on gerontological social work, this book includes a comprehensive array of topics within a single text. It discusses the important consideration of human behavior in the social environment context as a foundation for undertaking a comprehensive assessment of older adults and designing interventions. *Social Work with Older Adults* includes the protocols for both traditional and nontraditional interventions, recognizing the amazing heterogeneity of the aging population. In many respects, it can be considered as "one-stop shopping" for content on gerontological social work. Content on diversity of gender, race, ethnicity, and sexual orientation is integrated into each chapter as it is relevant to the topic, rather than being isolated in a separate chapter. This approach helps students to incorporate the importance of cultural sensitivity as an issue is being discussed, rather than doing so retrospectively.

The Plan of the Book

Chapter 1 begins with a demographic overview of the population of older adults as they look in the early twenty-first century and as they will look 20 years from now as baby boomers move into old age. This chapter describes the variety of social and medical settings in which gerontological social work is practiced including both clinical and macro settings. A substantial portion of the chapter is devoted to the personal and professional challenges of working with this population. Chapter 2 presents an in-depth look at the physical changes that accompany the normal aging process as well as full descriptions of the unique challenges presented to older adults faced with incontinence or HIV/AIDS. This chapter also presents the findings of the MacArthur Study and the Harvard Adult Development Study, the largest research studies ever designed to identify those factors associated with "successful" aging. Chapter 3 addresses the psychosocial patterns of adjustment observed in older adults, including those factors that contribute to delaying cognitive and intellectual losses and preventing social isolation. The chapter also includes a discussion of the differences between prescriptive and descriptive social theories of aging.

Chapter 4 moves the student into the mechanics of the assessment process, building on the didactic and theoretical content of the previous chapter, including determining the purpose of an assessment, the components of a comprehensive assessment, tools for assessing cognitive and socioemotional characteristics, and the special adaptations necessary in working with older adults. Differential assessment and diagnosis of the most common socioemotional and cognitive problems associated with aging, including depression, dementia, delirium, and anxiety, are presented in Chapter 5. Case studies are presented to help students sharpen their assessment skills in differentiating these conditions. Traditional treatment approaches, such as cognitive-behavioral therapy, validation therapy, reminiscence, life review, and group work, are explored in Chapter 6. Alternative approaches for work with both high- and low-functioning older adults—using music, art, massage, therapeutic recreation, and pets—are explored in Chapter 7.

Alcohol and drug abuse among older adults is covered in Chapter 8 with specific attention to designing interventions that recognize the experiences of both lifelong and late-onset addiction problems. This chapter also addresses the alarming problem of high suicide rates among older adults who suffer from both untreated depression and long-standing substance abuse problems. Chapter 9 examines the problem of older adult abuse and neglect and the social worker's role in assessing abuse including a brief case history that illustrates a common ethical dilemma for social workers regarding self-neglect in older adults. Chapter 10 is devoted entirely to the importance of spirituality and religion in the lives of older adults and describes incorporating assessment and intervention techniques, such as the spiritual genogram, eco-map, and timeline, into traditional practice approaches. This chapter also includes the importance of the social work practitioner's developing awareness of his or her own spirituality. Chapter 11 discusses the social worker's role in end-of-life care, dying, bereavement, and the issue of advance directives, a powerful tool to empower persons of all ages to be more active in making end-of-life decisions. A consideration of how older adults' support systems can be mobilized in designing interventions follows in Chapter 12 including an in-depth discussion of the issue of grandparents raising grandchildren, a growing concern for the field of gerontological social work. Chapter 13 presents detailed material on the income support programs, health insurance options, and housing programs that exist for older adults. The chapter also helps students learn how to identify the specific support services available to older adults in their area of the country. Although most of the book is directed at assessing older adults and their specific needs, this chapter helps students identify the services that exist to meet those needs.

Acknowledgments

I would like to thank those who reviewed the third edition of this text and for their comments on ways to improve the text for this latest fourth edition. I'd like to thank: Elizabeth Danto, Hunter College; Carolyn Tice, University of Maryland–Baltimore County; Jonathan Alex, Lehman College; Patricia Kolar, University of Pittsburgh; Stacey Kolomer, University of Georgia; Brian Flynn, Binghamton University; and Bruce Friedman, California State University–Bakersfield.

Special thanks go to my own students at the Boston College Graduate School of Social Work, who were brutally honest about what they did and did not like about using the third edition as a text in the Social Work with Older Adults course. These students shared the challenges they faced as practitioners in the field as well as their own experiences with aging parents and grandparents. Teaching is the greatest joy of academic life and often the most humbling.

My deepest gratitude goes to my husband, Bill Dittrich, who has been so very patient and supportive over all these many years. His love is the anchor in my life. As Robert Browning said so eloquently, "Grow old along with me, the best is yet to be."

K. M.-D.

1

The Context of Social Work Practice with Older Adults

AGING IN THE TWENTY-FIRST CENTURY

One of the greatest challenges of the twenty-first century will be the tremendous increase in the number of older adults in both the United States and throughout the world. By 2030 when most baby boomers (those born between 1946 and 1964) have moved into older adulthood one in every five persons in the United States will be over the age of 65. Social institutions, including the health-care system, education, income maintenance and social insurance programs, the workplace, and particularly social services, are bound to be radically transformed by these staggering numbers. Current and future generations of older adults will undoubtedly forge new approaches to the aging process itself and demand services that reflect positive and productive approaches to this time in their lives. As major providers of service to older adults and their families, social workers need a wide variety of skills and resources to meet these demands. Working with older adults is the fastest-growing segment of the social work profession. The National Institute on Aging estimates that between 60,000 and 70,000 new social workers will be needed to meet the demands of this growing population. This book is intended to provide a solid knowledge base about aging as a process and to introduce practitioners to a broad range of assessment and intervention techniques.

Diversity within the Older Adult Population

Age 65 is generally agreed on as the beginning of older adulthood only because until recently it has been the traditional retirement age, not because there is a special social or biological reason for this choice. The population between 65 and 74 is generally referred to as the "young-old." Many young-old do not consider themselves to be old. The young-old may still be working or newly retired, have few if any health problems, and remain actively engaged in the social activities of life. These older adults may stay in the labor market for many years beyond retirement age or

Competencies Applied with Practice Behaviors Examples —In This Chapter

- ☑ Professional Identity
- ☑ Ethical Practice
- ☐ Critical Thinking
- ☐ Diversity in Practice
- ☑ Human Rights & Justice
- ☐ Research-Based Practice
- ☐ Human Behavior
- ☐ Policy Practice
- ☐ Practice Contexts
- ☐ Engage, Assess, Intervene, Evaluate

transfer their energy and interests to creative writing, painting, music, or travel. They are most likely to continue to be engaged in their communities through volunteer work or political involvement.

The group of older adults aged 75 to 85, "the middle-old," may begin to experience health problems more frequently than their younger cohort. They may face some mobility restrictions and are more likely to openly identify as older adults. Most of these older adults are out of the workforce and may have experienced the loss of a life-partner or spouse. There is often a growing need for some type of supportive service to help these older adults remain in their own homes, if that is what they choose to do. It is among the "oldest old," those over 85, that the greatest needs exist. This group is most likely to have serious health problems and need assistance in more than one personal care area, such as bathing, eating, dressing, toileting, or walking. The needs of newly retired and healthy older adults to continue active and productive lifestyles are appreciably different from the needs of frail older adults forced into special living situations due to failing health. Somewhere in between the newly retired and frail older adults is the largest group of older adults, those who remain independent and function well in most areas of their lives but need specific social, health, or mental health services to maintain and maximize that independence.

Culture, ethnic group membership, gender, life experiences, and sexual orientation add to the uniqueness of the aging experience for each older adult. Some older adults have struggled with racial, gender, or sex discrimination throughout their adult years, factors that have a long-term effect on their socioeconomic well-being. Others bring significant health-care problems into old age, the result of inadequate health care since childhood. The dramatic rise in the number of divorces and fewer traditional family structures have created a complex web of blended families, stepchildren, multiple grandparents, and former spouses and partners expanding (and limiting) the support systems available to help an individual. Some older adults are "tech smart" while others have not had the opportunity or resources to access digital technology. While some older adults have used traditional social services at other times in their lives, many have never had to seek help until they reached their later years. The social work profession's commitment to recognizing and valuing the uniqueness of every individual is especially important in work with this population as will become apparent throughout this book.

The Focus of This Chapter

This chapter is designed to introduce you to the demographic characteristics of older adults in the United States. This chapter also describes the variety of professional social work roles both as direct service providers and in macro-level settings. Direct service roles include work in community social service settings, home health-care agencies, geriatric case management, independent and assisted-living communities, adult day health settings, nursing homes, and hospitals. New social work roles are being defined in legal settings and in the field of preretirement planning. Macro-level roles include local, state, and regional planning; legislative advocacy; public education; research; education; and consultancy in business and industry. These roles will be explored in depth later in this chapter along with the unique challenges that make this area of social work practice both rewarding and challenging.

THE DEMOGRAPHY OF AGING

The Growth of the Older Population

As of 2009, one in eight Americans was over the age of 65, or 12.9 percent of the general population (Administration on Aging, 2010). By 2030, when the last of the baby boomer cohort reaches age 65, older adults will comprise over 20 percent of Americans, or 72 million people (U.S. Census Bureau, 1996) (see Figure 1.1.). The largest growth within the older population will be among those over the age of 85, those older adults with the greatest health and social service needs.

The most notable growth in the older population will be among older adults of color, who will constitute 25 percent of the older adult population by 2030, as compared to 18 percent in 2000 (Federal Interagency Forum on Aging-Related Statistics, 2010) (see Figure 1.2). This growth is due to improvements in childhood health care—increasing the likelihood that persons of color will even reach age 65—and improvements in the control and treatment of infectious diseases throughout the life cycle. Yet, the consequences of a lifetime of economic challenge combined with a greater probability of developing chronic health problems will follow these older adults into this longer life expectancy. For older adults of color, living longer does not directly translate into living better. The special problems and challenges of growing older as a person of color are recurrent themes throughout this book.

Life Expectancy and Marital Status

A child born in 2007 can expect to live to 77.9 years of age, compared to a life expectancy of 47.3 years for a child born at the beginning of the twentieth century (National Center for Health Statistics, 2011). Women have a life expectancy of 80.4 years compared to

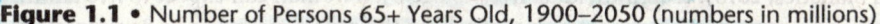

Figure 1.1 • Number of Persons 65+ Years Old, 1900–2050 (numbers in millions)

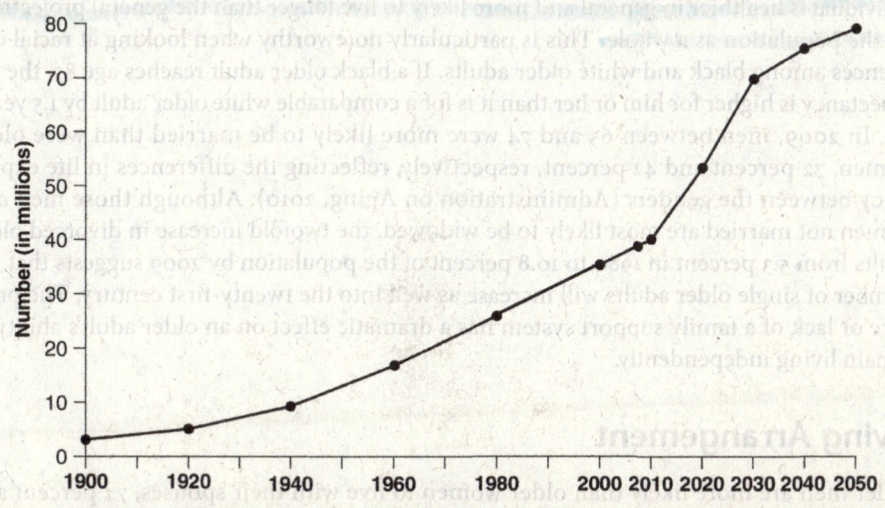

Sources: U.S. Bureau of the Census, *Population Projections of the United States by Age, Sex, Race and Hispanic Origin, 1995–2050,* Table G, Percent Distribution by Age 1990–2050 Current Population Reports, P25-1130, 1996; Census data 1900–1990.

Figure 1.2 • Percent of Population over 65 Years: By Race and Hispanic Origin, 2006 and 2050

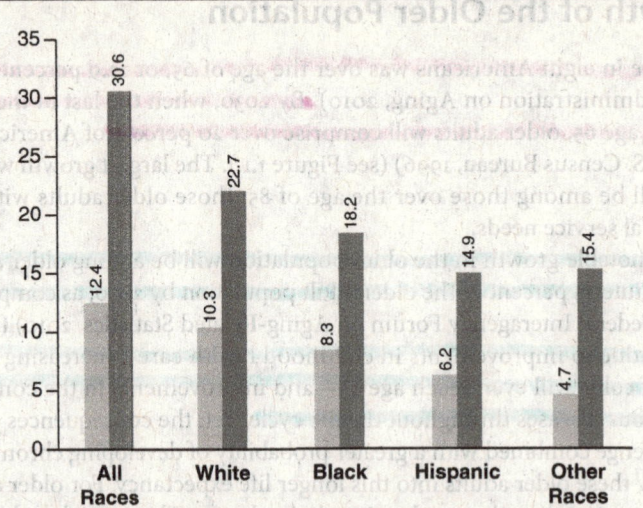

Sources: Data for 2006 are from the Administration on Aging (2006). *A Profile of Older Americans, 2006.* Washington, D.C.: U.S. Department of Health and Human Services. Data for 2050 are from the U.S. Bureau of the Census, *Population Projections of the United States by Age, Sex, Race and Hispanic Origin, 1993–2050,* Current Population Reports, P25-1104, 1993.

75.4 years for men. The projection of life expectancy changes as individuals get older. In other words, under current mortality conditions, if an individual lives until age 65, he or she can expect to live an average of 18.5 more years (Federal Interagency Forum on Aging-Related Statistics, 2010). If an individual lives to age 85, a woman can expect to live another 6.8 years and a man another 5.7 years. Just reaching the milestones of 65 or 85 suggests the individual is healthier in general and more likely to live longer than the general projections for the population as a whole. This is particularly noteworthy when looking at racial differences among black and white older adults. If a black older adult reaches age 85, the life expectancy is higher for him or her than it is for a comparable white older adult by 1.5 years.

In 2009, men between 65 and 74 were more likely to be married than were older women, 72 percent and 42 percent, respectively, reflecting the differences in life expectancy between the genders (Administration on Aging, 2010). Although those men and women not married are most likely to be widowed, the twofold increase in divorced older adults from 5.3 percent in 1980 to 10.8 percent of the population by 2009 suggests that the number of single older adults will increase as well into the twenty-first century. The presence or lack of a family support system has a dramatic effect on an older adult's ability to remain living independently.

Living Arrangement

Older men are more likely than older women to live with their spouses, 72 percent and 40.7 percent, respectively (Administration on Aging, 2010). Women are twice as likely to live alone than older men. This difference reflects the differences in life expectancy with older women being more likely to have outlived their spouses than older men. One of the most significant shifts in living arrangements for older adults in recent years is the increase in the number of grandparents raising grandchildren. Often this is due to death or disability of the older adults' grown children. Approximately 716,000 grandparents over the age of 65 were the head of households in which grandchildren lived, with two-thirds of these grandparents bearing the primary financial and child-rearing responsibilities (Administration on Aging, 2010). These numbers are proportionately higher among African-American and American Indian or Alaska Native and Hispanic older adults, populations already at risk for being low income and in poorer health. This increase in the number of grandparents raising grandchildren presents a formidable challenge in terms of meeting the parenting needs of the children at a time when the older adult's economic and personal resources are often challenged by their own needs.

In 2009, 56.5 percent of older adults lived in just 11 states: California, Florida, New York, Texas, Pennsylvania, Ohio, Illinois, Michigan, North Carolina, Georgia, and New Jersey. Thirty percent of older adults lived in areas considered "central cities," with 53 percent living in suburban areas. The remaining one-fifth of older adults lived in small cities and rural areas, those areas of the country most likely to have fewer health and social services available to the aging population (Federal Interagency Forum on Aging-Related Statistics, 2010).

Although 90 percent of nursing home residents are over the age of 65, they represent only 4.1 percent of the older population, according to the Administration on Aging (2010). This small percentage challenges the common perception that large numbers of older adults end up in nursing homes due to failing health. Women comprise 75 percent of the nursing home population, another reflection of their longer life expectancy (National Center for Health Care Statistics, 2011).

Poverty

The change from Old Age Assistance to Supplemental Security Income in 1972 and the expansion of government-funded health-care programs for older adults have reduced the overall poverty of older adults since the 1960s, when 35 percent of persons over the age of 65 had incomes below the poverty line (Federal Interagency Forum on Aging-Related Statistics, 2010). In 2009, 10.7 percent of older women and 6.6 percent of older men still had incomes that categorized them as poor (National Women's Law Center, 2010). A closer look at the poverty statistics indicates that individuals who have low incomes throughout their working lives are those most likely to continue to have low incomes or drop into poverty in their later years. Older women are more likely to be widowed or living alone than are their male counterparts—thus relying on one income, rather than two. However, poverty is not a new experience for many women. Women experience higher poverty rates throughout their lives whether due to the financial demands of raising children as single mothers, disrupted labor market histories, or low-wage occupational choices (National Women's Law Center, 2010).

There are disproportionately high poverty rates among older adults of color, with 19.5 percent of African-American older adults showing incomes below the poverty line. Hispanic and Asian/Pacific Islander older adults have poverty rates of 18.3 and 15.8 percent, respectively (Administration on Aging, 2010). The low lifetime earnings of both women and persons of color are reflected in lower Social Security benefits after retirement (National Women's Law Center, 2010). Limited incomes do not enable individuals to accumulate assets, such as property or personal savings accounts, and low-wage jobs rarely have pension or retirement plans. When a low-wage worker retires, he or she simply does not have the financial resources to ensure an income much above the poverty line. On the other hand, high-wage workers have higher Social Security payments, have greater asset accumulation, and are more likely to have private pensions or employer-supported retirement savings. Older adults' retirement incomes mirror their lifetime earnings.

Employment

About 16.2 percent of the current population of older adults remains in the workforce beyond the traditional retirement age of 65, with over half working part time either out of financial necessity or because of a continued interest in employment (Administration on Aging, 2010; Bureau of Labor Statistics, 2010). Baby boomers are expected to remain in the workforce at much higher numbers than the current cohort of older adults, with "more than three-quarters of boomers seeing work as playing some part in their retirement" (Merrill Lynch, 2005, p. 1). However, these workers are likely to seek "bridge jobs," those employment arrangements that allow them to work fewer hours with more workplace flexibility as they transition into full retirement (Cahill, Giandrea, & Quinn, 2006). Changes in the retirement age under Social Security, the decrease in the number of guaranteed retirement pensions, and a decrease in the amount of private savings for retirement contribute to both the interest in and necessity of baby boomers remaining connected to the workforce longer (Munnell, Webb, & Delorme, 2006).

Health Status and Disability

By age 85, over half of older adults need some assistance with mobility, bathing, preparing meals, or some other activity of daily living (Centers for Disease Control and Prevention & The Merck Foundation, 2007). However, in 2009, three-quarters of persons between ages 65 and 74 and two-thirds of persons over age 75 self-rated their health as good or very good (Administration on Aging, 2010), despite a high incidence of chronic health conditions within this population. Heart disease, arthritis, cancer, cerebrovascular disease, chronic obstructive pulmonary disease, and diabetes are the most frequent chronic health conditions found in persons over the age of 65 (Federal Interagency Forum on Aging-Related Statistics, 2010). Older adults are more likely than their nonaged counterparts to visit a physician or enter a hospital, which is consistent with the prevalence of chronic health-care problems.

Economic well-being and health status are intricately linked in the population. Chronic poverty restricts access to quality medical care, contributes to malnutrition, and creates psychological stress, all of which influence an individual's health status. For low-income older adults of color, late life becomes the manifestation of a lifetime of going without adequate medical care. Chronic conditions become more disabling. Prescriptions cannot be filled or glasses purchased because of limited financial resources. Poor older adults may have to choose between food and medicine.

The economic burden of an acute or chronic illness can devastate middle-class older adults' financial resources, quickly moving them from economic security to poverty. Much of this is due to the mechanics of financing health care for older adults. Medicaid, the health insurance program for low-income persons, is available to those older adults who qualify on the basis of low income and limited assets. Low-income older adults may be eligible to combine Medicaid coverage with Medicare, the federal health insurance program that covers 95 percent of persons over age 65 and does not have a means test. With the combination of both programs, most major health-care costs are covered, although accessibility to health-care services may still be a problem for low-income older adults (Administration on Aging, 2010). Medicare covers only a portion of health-care costs for older adults and is not sufficient to provide adequate coverage. For middle- and upper-income older adults, Medicare is frequently supplemented with what are known as *medigap* policies—private insurance that covers what Medicare does not. For those older adults who do not qualify for Medicaid and cannot afford supplemental policies, a significant gap in coverage exists. The National Center for Health Statistics estimates that almost 10 percent of older adults, most of whom are poor, female, and of color, have unmet health-care needs due in part to the gaps in the Medicare system (National Center for Health Care Statistics, 2011). This population is least likely to have routine physical exams, be immunized against the flu and pneumonia, have early screening for diabetes and hypertension, or take medications that prevent the development of more serious medical conditions. Therefore, when illness occurs, it is more likely to be serious. Prevention costs less than treatment for most chronic conditions, but a portion of the older population cannot afford preventative measures.

This overview of the demographics of aging shows a population of persons over the age of 65 that is growing and will continue to grow rapidly during the twenty-first century. Despite a higher incidence of chronic health problems, most older adults are not sick, not poor, and not living in nursing homes. The vast majority of older adults struggle with occasional health problems but continue to be active, involved, and productive members of society, defying the stereotype of sick, isolated, and miserable old people. The economic picture, however, is bleakest for older adults of color, women, and the oldest of the old in the United States. If current trends continue, older adults will continue to live longer but not necessarily healthier lives unless chronic poverty and health-care inadequacies are addressed.

USING THE STRENGTHS PERSPECTIVE IN WORK WITH OLDER ADULTS

The demographic overview of the older adults may leave you wondering how the social work profession can even begin to help this population, which faces so many problems with limited income and chronic health problems. If a social worker focuses on all the things that are "wrong" in an older adult's life, the challenges are indeed overwhelming both to the social worker and the older adult. This book uses the strengths perspective, which focuses on what is "strong" in an older adult's ability to rally personal and social assets to find solutions to the problems he or she faces in the aging process. The strengths perspective is based on the philosophy that building on strengths, rather than problems and personal liabilities, "facilitates hope and self-reliance" (Fast & Chapin, 2000, p. 7). To work effectively with older adults, the social worker has to believe that older adults continue to have the power to grow and change as they face challenges of aging and that they want and need to continue to be involved in decisions and choices about their care.

[Handwritten margin notes: Medicare — "No means test" means for ALL of us. Entitlements comes through social security. Medicaid — for people of low incomes. "means test" comes through social services]

The focus of this book is on very specific challenges facing older adults, including health and mental health issues, substance abuse, abuse and neglect, family relationships, and end-of-life issues, but incorporates the strengths perspective as an underlying theoretical approach to practice. The strengths perspective focuses on the ways in which clients have overcome challenges throughout their lives using a broad repertoire of coping and problem-solving skills (Glicken, 2004). An older adult who is experiencing the difficult decision to sell a much cherished family home and move into independent or assisted living has had to make painful decisions before and found the inner strength and social support to do so. An older adult struggling with a late-onset drinking problem has the physical and emotional ability to overcome an unhealthy reliance on alcohol. The strengths perspective affirms a basic tenet of social work practice: self-determination. If the social worker sets the goals for an intervention and those goals are not those of the older adult, the worker should not be surprised when the older adult is resistant or uncooperative. "Clients create change, not helpers" (Glicken, 2004, p. 5). The social worker's roles are to help older adults identify strengths, resources, and goals, connect the older adult with personal and community resources to meet those goals, and facilitate and coordinate the process, if necessary. You will see how this approach is used throughout the book in specific areas of gerontological social work. There are other excellent resources that present the strengths perspective in more detail and you are encouraged to consult those sources for a more in-depth discussion of this approach (Fast & Chapin, 2000; Glicken, 2004; Saleebey, 1992).

SETTINGS FOR GERONTOLOGICAL SOCIAL WORK

You work with them — Everywhere!

Older adults' need for social services falls along a broad continuum from the need for a limited number of support services such as housekeeping and meal services to extensive needs in a long-term or rehabilitation setting. Likewise, social workers' roles range from the traditional assistance as broker, advocate, case manager, or therapist to nontraditional roles such as exercise coach, yoga teacher, and spiritual counselor. Nursing homes and hospitals are often seen as the most familiar settings for gerontological social work practice, but these settings represent a small part of the variety of opportunities available for social workers with passion for and knowledge about the older adult population. With only 4.1 percent of the older population in nursing homes, social service agencies, home health-care agencies, geriatric care management, adult day health, and independent and assisted-living settings are more common settings for direct service or clinical practice. Social work roles in legal settings and in the expanding field of preretirement planning are additional settings for gerontological social work that function in a complementary role to the existing social service system. Social workers serve important roles in macro-level settings that serve older adults such as community organizations and public education, local, state, and regional planning agencies, and organizations that engage in legislative advocacy. The future roles of social workers in the field of aging are limited only by practitioners' imagination and initiative.

Community Social Service Agencies

In large communities, social service agencies offer a wide range of counseling, advocacy, case management, and protective services specifically designed for older adults. These services may be housed in the local Council on Aging, Area Agency on Aging, or Department of Social Services, or may be provided by sectarian agencies, such as Catholic Social Services, Lutheran Social Services, Jewish Family and Children's Services, and so forth. Older adults or their families may feel more confident working with agencies that reflect their own religious affiliation. In small communities or rural areas, services to older adults may be contained within a regional agency that serves as an Area Agency on Aging (AAA) or an agency serving other populations that has a social worker with particular expertise in working with older adults. The purpose and organization of AAAs will be discussed in detail in Chapter 13.

Contact with a social worker at a social service agency is frequently initiated by a concerned family member who is unsure about how to begin the process of obtaining services for a family member. In addition to conducting the assessment process to determine what services might be helpful to an older adult, social workers can play an important role in initiating and coordinating services from a variety of agencies in a care management role. In some cases, the family of a frail older adult becomes the client. Although families can successfully provide caregiving, they may feel the strain of this responsibility and benefit from a support or educational group and respite services. As the contact is often precipitated by a crisis, families and older adults may need reassurance and support as well as solid information to stabilize a chaotic situation.

Home Health-Care Agencies

Home health-care agencies, such as the Visiting Nurses Association, often have gerontological social workers on staff as part of a team approach to providing services to older adults. Although the primary focus of home health care is to provide health-related services, such as checking blood pressure, changing dressings following surgery, or monitoring blood sugar levels for diabetic older adults, social workers can also play an important role in addressing older adults' psychosocial needs. An older adult who has suffered a stroke may not only need medication and blood pressure monitoring from a health-care provider but also need help with housekeeping, meal preparation, or transportation. The social worker can arrange for these support services and coordinate the total care plan. Older adults who are essentially homebound due to chronic health problems often experience intense isolation and may benefit from regular phone calls from an older adult call service or friendly visitor volunteer. Gerontological social workers who work in home health care often provide supportive or psychotherapeutic counseling services or arrange for those services from another agency in the community.

Social workers also play an important role in helping older adults work out the financial arrangements for home health care. Advocating for the older adults to receive the care they are entitled to under private insurance, Medicare, or Medical Assistance can involve myriad phone calls and personal contacts that are difficult for an ill older adult to handle. When older adults are not eligible for needed services under existing insurance coverage, creativity is often needed to obtain additional financial resources, including working with older adults' families or identifying low-cost community services that older adults can afford. If an older adult's illness becomes more debilitating, the social worker may need to work with the older adult to identify care arrangements that offer greater support, such as assisted-living services or adult day health care. It is the social worker's knowledge of community services and financial aid programs that makes him or her a valuable asset to home health care.

Geriatric Care Management

Families in the twenty-first century are increasingly juggling the demands of full-time employment, hectic family schedules, and geographical separation from aging family members. An option available to families who may not have the time, knowledge, or availability to negotiate with community social services agencies or home health-care agencies is that of using a geriatric care manager. Geriatric care management has emerged as one of the newest and most rapidly growing professional settings for gerontological social work.

Most geriatric care managers are social workers, nurses, or other specially trained counseling or health-care workers who may work as independent professionals or in conjunction with a health-care facility or social service agency. Geriatric care managers offer family members or other caregivers services in planning, implementing, and coordinating a wide range of services for older adults (National Association of Professional Geriatric Care Managers, 2011). These professionals have a specialized knowledge in assessing the biopsychosocial needs of an older adult and in locating the appropriate service in the community to meet those needs.

The overall responsibilities of the geriatric care manager are to suggest the most appropriate supportive services needed to enhance the older adult's well-being. This may be as simple as arranging for health-monitoring services for an older adult who is recuperating from surgery or as complex as relocating the older adult to an assisted-living facility or a nursing home (Stone, Reinhard, Machemer, & Rudin, 2002). Geriatric care managers provide assessments and screening, arrange and monitor in-home help, provide supportive counseling to the older adult and the family, support crisis intervention, and even offer family mediation and conflict resolution when families have opposing views of what an aging parent needs or wants. They may also act as liaisons to families separated by long distances to report on the older adult's well-being or alert the family when an older adult's physical, psychological, financial, or social health changes.

The cost of geriatric care management can be substantial, with fees running between $60 and $90 per hour, depending on the type, complexity, and location of the services provided and the credentials of the care manager (National Association of Professional Geriatric Care Managers, 2011). These care management fees are typically not covered by Medicare, Medicaid, or traditional private health insurance, although the cost of the support services identified by the care manager are often part of the home health-care services financed by public and private health insurance programs.

Independent and Assisted-Living Settings

Specialized independent living settings for older adults in the community, such as low-income or moderate-income housing, frequently have social workers on staff to provide a variety of services. Helping older adults secure transportation to appointments or shopping centers, arranging opportunities for social activities such as plays and concerts, and promoting on-site activities are frequently under the auspices of a social worker in an independent living center. The social worker may be instrumental in helping the older adult to make the decision to add additional home care services or transition to a housing setting that offers more support as the older adult's needs change with changing health conditions.

Another option in the range of services available to older adults in the community is the assisted-living center. *Assisted living* is defined as a residential, long-term arrangement designed to promote maximum independent functioning among frail older adults while providing in-home support services (Assisted Living Federation of America, 2011). The assisted-living model fits in between completely independent living and the intensive care provided in a skilled nursing home. Some assisted-living facilities are part of a larger complex known as a continuum of care facility. Older adults may purchase or rent an apartment while they are still completely independent. As their health changes, necessitating increasing levels of support, older adults may need to move within the same complex to semi-independent living and perhaps eventually into an adjacent skilled nursing facility.

It should be noted that the quality and quantity of services available to older adults to support independent living varies widely among assisted-living facilities (Assisted Living Federation of America, 2011). Although some facilities are more accurately described as "real estate commodities with food service and social activities," others are comprehensive health-care settings offering a wide range of physical, health, and social supports that truly do offer seniors healthy, high-quality care (Franks, 2002, p. 13). The assisted-living industry does not require nor regulate the use of professional social workers, although positions such as the care or service coordinator utilize the skills associated with professional social work practice.

In high-quality assisted-living facilities, the focus is on as much self-maintenance as possible for each resident. Residents live in private or semiprivate rooms that have a private bathroom and, in some facilities, a small kitchen. The monthly fees include rent, utilities, a meal plan, and housekeeping services. Other services such as laundry, personal care services, and transportation are provided on an individual basis as part of a total care plan. Assisted living is expensive, usually between $3000 and $5000 a month, making it affordable only for middle- and upper-income older adults (Metlife Mature Market Institute, 2006). However, some states are working to obtain Medicaid waivers to demonstrate the cost-saving effect of using the assisted-living model for low-income persons as opposed to placing these older adults in skilled nursing facilities (Salmon, Polivka, & Soberson-Ferrer, 2006).

The purpose of assisted living is to help older adults maintain and improve their psychosocial functioning through a variety of activities that maximize choice and control. Social workers conduct intake assessments to review the medical, functional, and psychological strengths and weaknesses of incoming residents. These assessments play an important role in identifying those areas in which an older adult may need supplementary services, such as chore services, assistance with bathing or dressing, or social activities to ease isolation.

Families and residents may need both information and support to make a successful transition to the facility. The decision to leave one's own home, even to move into the privacy of an apartment, is a traumatic experience for older adults and may require professional support to work through the grief and depression (Edelman, Guihan, Bryant, & Monroe, 2006). Assisted-living centers can offer a variety of challenging social and recreational activities that help older adults make the center their new home. Helping a resident find the right balance between private time and social activities is another important role for a social worker in this setting. In assisted-living centers, social workers often function as part of a multidisciplinary team composed of nurses and occupational, physical, and recreational therapists (Vinton, 2004).

Adult Day Health Care

A setting for older adult care that falls between independent living and skilled nursing care is adult day health care. Adult day health care can provide individually designed programs of medical and social services for frail older adults who need structured care for some portion of the day. Older adults who live with their families or other caretakers or even live in semi-independent living situations and have some physical, cognitive, emotional, or social disability are typical users of adult day health care. These older adults do not need full-time nursing care or even full-time supervision but do require assistance with some of the activities of daily living. This type of care provides a valuable role as respite care for caregivers as well. Adult children may be willing and able to have older adults live with them if they can obtain supplementary care during the day while they work or for occasional respite (National Adult Day Services Association, 2011).

Many adult day health centers only take older adults who are able to be active participants in the development of their own service plans and consent to placement in the adult day health center. This type of care focuses on maximizing an older adult's sense of choice and control in their own care. A smaller number of centers work exclusively with older adults who suffer from dementia, including Alzheimer's disease, who may be less able to be full participants in the decision-making process.

Social workers are involved with an older adult from the extensive preplacement process through the execution of a service plan. Social workers and older adults explore the older adult's needs and interests together and select from a variety of rehabilitative and recreational services available at the adult day health center. An older adult may need physical or occupational therapy to compensate for losses due to a stroke or heart attack. Others may need supervision to take medication. The social worker in adult day health care is instrumental in coordinating all the physical needs frail older adults require during the day. In this setting, social workers may serve as care managers.

Group work is an essential role for social workers in adult day health centers. In most centers, older adults belong to a specific group that meets on a regular basis to talk about the issues they face. This may involve problems with families and caregivers, concerns about friends and members of the group, or more structured topics such as nutrition, foot care, or arthritis. The group becomes a focal point for older adults in the adult day health setting. It gives them an opportunity to maintain social skills or renew them if they have been socially isolated. The group is helpful in making new older adults feel welcome and helping them access all of the services available to them.

In addition to running a therapeutic group and a variety of social and recreational activities, the social worker meets individually with each older adult for counseling, advocacy, or problem solving. This individual attention plays an important role in maintaining the dignity of the older adult in what is predominately a group setting and in helping the worker monitor the older adult's mental and physical health status. At times, older adults may be reluctant to share deeply personal issues such as family problems, depression, and incontinence with members of their group and benefit more from a private discussion with the social worker.

When older adults are not meeting with their group or social worker, they are usually involved in a wide variety of activity groups geared to their special interests. Physical fitness, music, education, current events, arts and crafts, and creative writing are among the types of groups found in adult day health centers.

Nursing Homes

One of the greatest fears of older adults is that they will end up living in a nursing home. This fear explains why older adults fight so hard to maintain their independence. Nursing homes are seen as a place older adults are sent to die, neglected and forgotten by their families. Although this fear may be legitimate for some older adults, nursing homes serve an important role in the continuum of care for frail older adults. When independent living becomes impossible and more structured nursing care is needed, a nursing home may be the most appropriate service.

With a growing older population, it would be expected that the number of nursing homes would be increasing proportionately. However, between 1995 and 2004, the actual number of nursing homes decreased by 16 percent. The number of beds has increased by 9 percent, meaning that today's nursing home is likely to be bigger than in previous years and that nursing home care is available in fewer locations (National Center for Health Care Statistics, 2004). The decrease in the overall number of nursing homes reflects the improvement in choices available to older adults for health care. Older adults are opting to stay in their own homes longer with the help of less-costly home-based alternatives to skilled nursing care.

The primary role of the social worker in a nursing home is to serve in both a supportive and an educational role to older adults and their families (Vourlekis & Simons, 2006). Social workers begin to work with older adults and their families prior to admission to a nursing home—arranging preadmission visits, doing a preliminary assessment of what kinds of services will best meet the needs of the older adult once admitted, and working out financial arrangements. Nursing home care can cost more than $6000 a month and is not routinely covered by private insurance or Medicare. (Metlife Mature Market Institute, 2006). Some older adults will spend only a few months in a skilled nursing facility—for instance, recovering from an acute illness or surgery—so the social worker's job may include discharge planning as well.

Nursing home social workers also assume a supportive role in their work with the friends and families of residents. Placing a family member in a nursing home frequently generates guilt and anxiety among family members. They may feel they are abandoning their older adults, despite the fact that less drastic measures have already failed. Maintaining the relationship with the resident, identifying resources for handling the financial demands of placement, and processing the conflicting feelings that accompany placement are common responsibilities for nursing home social workers.

Hospitals *they think "Hospitals - leads to the grave"*

Over one-third of hospital admissions are persons over the age of 65, and this population used 44 percent of the total days of care in the hospital setting (DeFrances & Podgornik, 2004) due primarily to the presence of chronic health-care problems in this population. The complexities of chronic health problems make hospital social work with older adults an essential part of the recovery process. Hospital social workers provide a wide variety of services, including crisis intervention, patient advocacy, patient education, family liaison work, care management, and discharge planning (Volland & Keepnews, 2006).

Hospitalization is a crisis for anyone of any age, but with older adults there is always the fear that the hospital is the gateway to either a nursing home or the grave. Older adults may be anxious about upcoming surgery or be lost in the maze of medical jargon they hear. They may be concerned about what happens to them during the recovery process when they return home by themselves. Families may be concerned that their loved ones will receive too little care or be hooked up to life-sustaining equipment against their will. In sum, the hospital setting can be a very chaotic environment for older adults and their families. Crisis counseling in a hospital setting involves helping the older adult and families reestablish an emotional equilibrium, begin to understand the medical condition, prioritize tasks, and develop a short-term action plan. The primary focus of the social worker is to help with the psychosocial needs of the older adult in the hospital setting while medical personnel attend to physical health.

Patient advocacy is another appropriate role for hospital social work with older adults. Older adults may find the cold, impersonal atmosphere of the hospital frightening and confusing. They may need help in making their needs known or advocating on their own behalf. For example, a Chinese woman may need a translator, require a special diet, or wish to meet with an herbal healer. Social workers can work with other health-care professionals to find the best match between what the client wants and what the health-care system can tolerate. A part of patient advocacy is patient education, working with older adults and their families to better understand the presenting illness and its course of treatment. Patient education is aimed at empowerment of the older adult. The more older adults know and understand about their illness, the better their own sense of control. When they feel they are part of the treatment process, they are more likely to be active participants in their own healing.

Social workers may also serve as family liaisons for the hospitalized older adult. The older adult's family needs to understand what is happening to the older adult, the prognosis for the illness, and what plans need to be made following the hospitalization. For many families, contact with a hospital social worker is the first contact they have had with the social services system. Up until that point, they may have struggled to provide care on their own, unaware of the range of community services available to them. The process of discharge planning, another important hospital social work role, involves developing and coordinating the support services for post-hospitalization. Meals-on-Wheels, home health care, chore services, and homemaking services can be very effective in helping older adults to maintain their independence while providing invaluable support.

Social workers can provide both educational and supportive presence in helping older adults and their families make difficult end-of-life decisions. Helping older adults make choices about what circumstances warrant being connected to life-support equipment, whether they want to be resuscitated after a heart attack, or who should make those choices when they are unable to are sensitive issues. Facilitating the discussion between an older adult and the family about these questions may be among the most difficult tasks in hospital social work.

DEVELOPING AREAS FOR DIRECT PRACTICE

Although social workers will be needed in the most traditional areas already discussed, there is unlimited potential for direct practice in other areas with older adults with the growth of this population. Two specific areas that will need a greater number of social workers are the legal services area and preretirement planning programs in both the public and private sectors.

Legal Services

Law and social work have had a long and sometimes tumultuous history. Although the professions share the joint goal of problem solving, the clash between legal and social work professions' foci in the resolution of problems is a major challenge to interprofessional cooperation. Whereas law uses strict interpretations of existing laws and legal precedents, the confines of administrative rules and regulations, and a much more factual, not feeling, approach to problems, social work's approach is more deeply rooted in the consideration of the biopsychosocial factors that influence the development and perpetuation of a problem facing a client (Madden & Wayne, 2003; Taylor, 2006). However, these professions can work together very effectively once each profession's expertise is clarified. This is particularly beneficial in areas of elder law. Helping an older adult and his or her family make provisions for Durable Powers of Attorney for Health Care or determine competency in the case of dementia are good examples of the necessity of social workers and lawyers working collaboratively. When an older adult is competent but needs assistance in managing property or finances, lawyers and social workers are both important members of a team that will set up (and explain) guardianship (Joslin & Fleming, 2001; Sember, 2008). Another example is when an older adult is facing a problem that has very distinct social and legal implications, such as housing. What may have started out as an occasional lapse in the older adult's ability to remember to pay the rent may escalate into an eviction proceeding. The immediate legal action necessary to halt the physical removal of the older adult from the residence is the lawyer's role. The social work role involves long-term solutions to the housing crisis, such as finding a way to pay back rent, identifying another party to act as a fiscal agent, or considering the move to a safer, more structured living situation. One of the fastest-growing areas of elder law is that of the legal issues facing grandparents raising grandchildren. Issues in custody of dependent grandchildren, financial support, and discrimination in housing lead the list of sociolegal challenges facing this population (National Academy of Elder Law Attorneys, 2011; Wallace, 2001). Lawyers are invaluable in navigating the complex system of child welfare law, whereas social workers are better prepared to handle the social and mental health challenges facing these older adults and their dependent grandchildren. The best solutions to these challenges will come only by interprofessional teamwork.

Preretirement Planning *How to afford / adjust retirement*

Preretirement planning often is equated with financial planning; however, an adequate income is only half of the challenge of retirement. It is easy to see how the demand for services in this area is growing as the first group of baby boomers is facing retirement. The area of preretirement planning that receives the least attention is the psychosocial aspect of the transition from full-time employment to whatever is next. For people who have defined themselves in terms of their jobs or have relied almost exclusively on the workplace for social contacts, retirement can be very challenging. What do people do now? How will they redefine their lives to create a balance between the joys of leisure activities and continued productivity? How will couples manage relationships when they are together all the time as opposed to having separate lives at work? Most important, what challenges face individuals who simply cannot afford to retire, even in the face of serious chronic health conditions? These questions embody the very essence of social work's expertise in the biopsychosocial dimensions of people's well-being. The social work profession is only now beginning to define its role in this process, usually in the context of Employee Assistance Programs available in both the public and private sector. The most exciting aspect of this area of practice is that the roles for social workers are yet to be clearly defined. How social workers can facilitate a healthy adjustment to retirement will be shaped by the next generation of gerontological social workers.

MACRO SETTINGS FOR GERONTOLOGICAL SOCIAL WORKERS

The role of social workers in direct service settings is readily apparent, but gerontological social workers also play an invaluable role in macro settings, such as community practice, planning, and legislative and political advocacy. The United States has a well-developed federal aging services and programs network, authorized by various titles of the Older Americans Act of 1965. These include an authorization for a national, regional, state, and local structure to plan and deliver a wide range of services to older adults as well as to systematically plan for the future needs of older adults and advocate on behalf of this population in the legislative setting. Some of the macro practice roles for social workers fall directly within this network. The aging services network and the programs it oversees will be discussed in detail in Chapter 13. Other gerontological social workers practice within private and community agencies specifically dedicated to the planning and legislative advocacy interests of older adults.

Community Practice

The major foci of community practice with older adults is to mobilize and empower the older adult population to take an active role in their own problem solving by emphasizing the shared concerns of a community, rather than solving one individual crisis at a time. Community work with older adults encompasses a wide variety of settings. *Community* can mean something as specific as a congregate housing setting or as broad as a city or town. In smaller community settings, organizers can be instrumental in mobilizing older adults to get improved public transit, organize a building crime watch network, or improve snow removal in front of a housing development (Massachusetts Senior Action, 2011). Social workers can also help mobilize older adults to petition a city government to grant a property tax exemption, improve access to health and social services through development of neighborhood centers, or develop an emergency plan for weather or health-related emergencies.

Public education is another function within the general category of community practice for macro social workers. For example, when Medicare Part D, the prescription drug program, was being implemented in 2006, older adults desperately needed simple, clear information about the program. Providing this education either on an individual level or within the context of a community setting was often the responsibility of a social worker, who had a strong knowledge base in all aspects of Medicare and was particularly sensitive to older adults' needs and concerns. Likewise, social workers are currently involved in offering educational campaigns about HIV/AIDS, fraud and financial abuse prevention, home safety, and advance directives, all of which are discussed later in this book. Public education is not just "telling" people what they need to know. It involves a comprehensive and understandable presentation of why the information is crucial and the patience to listen to the questions and concerns of older adults.

Planning

Social workers also practice in the planning offices of State Offices on Aging and Area Agencies on Aging. Social planning involves the process of exploring both community needs and assets, developing plans of action, and evaluating future and existing policies and programs (Wacker & Roberto, 2008). The answer to the growing population of aging baby boomers is not to simply build lots of new senior centers. The real crisis lies in areas such as developing alternative housing, health, and leisure programs that reflect the needs of a very different generation of older adults. Planning involves comprehensive needs assessment, an in-depth understanding of changing demographics, and sensitivity to how new and existing services will be financed. How do the needs of urban older adults differ from those of suburban older adults? What kinds of emergency programs need to be designed to adequately protect older adults in case of natural disaster, a health epidemic, or weather crisis? What kinds of programs need to be developed to meet the needs of older adults who still need to work but require more flexible work arrangements or training to keep up with technological advances? These are the challenges to public planning officers who must not only know what is currently working but what will be needed in the future.

Legislative and Political Advocacy

Advocacy and empowerment are central tenets of the social work profession, both in their role of acting on behalf of individuals and on behalf of specific vulnerable client populations in the political arena. Most programs and services for older adults are funded by federal and state funds and thus require both supporting legislation and administrative authority to operate. The social work role in legislative advocacy involves creating public awareness among older adults about pending legislation that may affect them and mobilizing this population to pressure legislators to act on their behalf. The legislative process is complex and may be confusing to older adults without access to the inside issues around the legislation. State chapters of the National Association of Social Workers (NASW) have rallied both member and client support for such issues as mental health coverage parity laws, loan forgiveness for social work education, immigration rights, age and gender discrimination, and property tax relief for older adults.

NASW's Political Action for Candidate Election (PACE), the political action arm of the organization, works on behalf of candidates whose views on a variety of social welfare issues support the organization's policy agenda. They support these candidates through fund-raisers, campaign contributions, and public endorsement of the candidates during the elective process (National Association of Social Workers, 2011). The social work profession's role in legislative and political advocacy is a combination of local, state, and national efforts, all aimed at advocating for and empowering clients who are directly affected by the policy framework affecting policies and programs.

PERSONAL AND PROFESSIONAL ISSUES IN WORK WITH OLDER ADULTS

Although deeply rewarding both personally and professionally, work with older adults requires a high level of self-awareness on the part of the social worker. In all intervention efforts, workers bring their own emotional baggage to the helping process. However, in gerontological work, the issues are more complex. Unlike social work practice in the areas of alcoholism, drug abuse, family dysfunction, or domestic violence—social problem areas that may or may not personally affect the worker—everyone must eventually face the experience of aging and death for themselves and their families. Aging is not a social problem; it is a developmental stage. The universality of the aging experience influences work with older adults on both a conscious and subconscious level. Among the most significant issues workers will face are the subtle influences of lifelong social and personal messages about ageism, countertransference of feelings toward older adults, and conflicting issues surrounding independence versus dependence.

Ageist Personal and Social Attitudes

The term *ageism* refers to the prejudices and stereotypes attributed to older persons based solely on their age (Butler, 1989). These stereotypes are usually negative and convey an attitude that older adults are less valuable as human beings, thus justifying inferior or unequal treatment. These attitudes develop early in life as children observe parental, media, and social attitudes toward older adults. Parents may unintentionally send the message that aging parents and grandparents are a nuisance to care for, demanding, needy, or unpleasant. Even simple comments, such as "I hope I never get like Grandma" or "Put me to sleep if I ever get senile," may be interpreted literally by children. Every time parents refer to aches and pains as "I must be getting old," the subtle message becomes clear that aging is destined to be painful and debilitating. Although ageism is an attitude that hinders everyone's ability to adjust to the normal changes of aging, it also serves a more destructive social justification. Ageism rationalizes pushing people out of the labor market in the name of maintaining productivity without much thought to what happens to people when their lives are no longer centered on work as an organizing principle. Ageism justifies segregated living arrangements, substandard medical care, and generally derogatory attitudes toward older adults. Blatantly racist or sexist comments and open discrimination would not be tolerated in today's business and social arenas, yet ageist attitudes and comments are rarely challenged.

Countertransference

Countertransference is defined as the presence of unrealistic and often inappropriate feelings by the social worker toward the older adult that distort the helping relationship (Nathan, 2010; Reidbord, 2010). The worker displaces feelings or attitudes onto the client based on a past relationship rather than on the real attributes of the older adult with whom he or she is working. Countertransference develops from two primary sources in working with older adults. Internalizing ageist attitudes reflected in society can lead a social worker to intensively dislike working with older adults because they are subconscious reminders of death and illness. On an unconscious level, the social worker may believe his or her work is wasted because the older adult will soon die, benefiting minimally from the social worker's time and attention. Countertransference can also develop when a social worker is unaware that positive or negative relationships from the past are distorting the present relationship.

For example, a young social worker is assigned to work with an older woman in identifying an appropriate assisted-living facility, a painful but necessary move for the older woman. When she goes to the woman's house, the older woman insists on serving cookies and tea to her and they end up visiting for several hours rather than attending to the task at hand. When her supervisor inquires as to the decision about assisted living, the young woman hesitates and responds that she thinks it is "mean" that the family is making her go to assisted living, that this older woman wants to stay in her home and maybe with enough services she could stay there. She hasn't actually had the discussion about which assisted-living facility the older woman might select as it is just too awkward to bring up the topic. After the supervisor explores the situation with the worker, it becomes apparent that the worker overheard her own mother arguing with her grandmother a few years ago about the same kind of decision. She remembers her grandmother saying "if I have to leave my house, I might as well just die!" which in fact she did shortly after moving into assisted living. The older woman struggling with the decision to leave her own home was a subconscious reminder to the social worker of a painful situation in her own life. In order to alleviate her own pain and guilt, the worker was trying to avoid her client facing the same situation. The worker's need to "save" the older adult may rob the older adult unintentionally of his or her self-respect and personal dignity. It is essential to explore issues in countertransference with supervisors.

Ageism and Death Anxiety

Internalized negative attitudes toward the process of aging and older adults contribute to a pervasive presence of "death anxiety" in contemporary society. Death anxiety is a highly agitated emotional response, invoked by reference to or discussion of death and dying (Peck, 2009). Working with older adults is a constant reminder to the social worker of the logical progression of the life cycle—from youth to aging and death. American society does not deal well with death or any discussion of death. Consider all the phrases used to avoid saying the word *death*, such as "passed on," "expired," "gone on to the next world," and many others not quite so polite.

Facing a variety of situations surrounding death is an inevitable part of work with older adults. Many older adults will admit that death does not frighten them as much when they are older as it did when they were younger. They see friends and family members dying. Throughout their lives, they have thought about what death means to them, whether they believe there is an afterlife, and what their lives have been all about. If they have escaped the discomfort of chronic medical problems, they consider themselves lucky. If they live with a disabling or painful condition, they may welcome death as an end to the physical discomfort. Older adults often want to talk about funeral arrangements or make plans for disposing of their personal possessions even when family members do not. Although older adults' families may cling to denial as a means of warding off a critically ill older adult's death, hospital policy may simultaneously ask the family to make difficult end-of-life decisions. All these issues are examples of how social work with older adults requires some level of comfort on the part of the social worker in acknowledging and processing death not only with clients but also in one's own work in self-awareness.

The Independence/Dependence Struggle

One of the most frequently stated goals older adults voice is their desire to maintain their independence for as long as possible. This desire coincides with the social work profession's commitment to promote self-determination and preserve the dignity of the individual. On the surface, there appears to be no conflict. In reality, as older adults require more and more support services and experience increasing difficulties in maintaining

The OA Always makes the final decision unless deemed by court!

independent living, tensions between older adults' desires and families' and social workers' perceptions of need are inevitable. A worker can appreciate the desperate efforts on the part of an older adult to stay in his or her own home. Yet when an older adult is struggling with stairs or a deteriorating neighborhood, and difficulties in completing the simple activities of daily living challenge the feasibility of that effort, professional and personal dilemmas abound. Who ultimately must make a decision about an older adult's ability to stay in his or her own home? Who decides that an older adult is showing poor judgment about financial decisions? When does Protective Services step in to remove an older adult from a family member's home due to neglect or abuse, despite the older adult's objections? When do the wishes of the family supersede the wishes of the older adult, or do they ever? These are difficult questions for which there are no simple answers.

While functioning an entire lifetime as an independent adult, a single illness can reduce an older adult to dependency more quickly than he or she can emotionally process. In an effort to counteract a diminished sense of self-esteem, older adults may fight dependency to the point that they put themselves in physical jeopardy rather than risk relying on others. They may act out, show extreme anger, or make excessive demands on both social workers and family members that cannot be met. Maintaining independence should be a critical goal of all gerontological social work, and throughout this book, various ways of promoting independence, even among the most disabled older adults, will be presented.

Other older adults react by assuming dependent roles sooner than they need to and become more passive and resistant than their physical condition warrants, assuming a kind of "learned helplessness." Rather than fighting for their own independence, they give up and willingly relinquish the decision-making issues in their own care. Although giving up their own rights to decision making may make case planning easier for workers and families, this situation lends itself to the development of other, more subtle problems. One of the fundamental concepts of social work practice is the importance of clients' choice of goals for intervention and their personal commitment to work on those goals, a basic tenet in adapting the strengths-based perspective discussed earlier in this chapter. For example, a social worker may decide an older adult needs to attend a senior center program to decrease personal isolation. Even though the older adult may agree so as not to offend the social worker and out of gratefulness for all the worker has done for the older adult, the older adult will not go to the senior center and participate if he or she does not want to go. The older adult may not blatantly refuse to go, but rather will make appropriate excuses for nonattendance. Although well intentioned, the social worker has decided on a goal for the older adult that is the social worker's goal, not the client's. It is not surprising that family and workers become frustrated when older adults find ways to avoid doing something that is not their goal in the first place.

The process of relinquishing independence is the beginning of a very delicate process, even among those older adults who are sincerely willing to let others make decisions for them. Older adults become reactors rather than actors in their lives. Perceiving that they have little control over their lives, older adults may fall into a deep depression and relinquish their will to live along with their independence. Families and caregivers, who perceive that older adults have given up even when they are capable of some independent activities, may react with anger and hostility. The social worker's role is to help the older adult and family find common ground that promotes self-determination and meets the need for services.

Self-Awareness and Supervision

The challenges of working with older adults within a societal context of ageist attitudes—which contribute to deeply seated fears about one's own aging and death—may seem a bit overwhelming at this point in the book, but there are resources for resolving these issues. Through developing self-awareness with professional supervision, social workers can effectively work through these issues. They are discussed early in the text because they should be clearly present in your mind as you study this field of practice. Developing self-awareness is a process that takes time and continues to challenge professionals throughout their careers. It may take a lifetime of working with older adults (and one's own relatives) to recognize your own personal triggers for problematic feelings.

Workers need to take a critical look at any concurrent challenges they are facing in their own lives that could contribute to professional problems. A social worker who is also balancing the demands of an aging spouse, parents, or grandparents may feel such excessive demands on his or her own resources that working effectively with older adults may not be possible. Although such experiences may be helpful to the worker in developing compassion for an older adult's family, it may be counterproductive in the intervention process.

The ability to keep feelings at a conscious level is one of the most important parts of the process of developing self-awareness in working with older adults. One's personal feelings toward a client, family members, and the quality of the professional relationship are important clues to the worker about his or her own emotional issues. Supervisors can be helpful in diversifying tasks for the worker in an effort to defuse the emotions generated by intense cases. Working exclusively with highly dependent older adults or those with Alzheimer's disease can tax even the most well-adjusted, experienced workers.

Most gerontological social workers, including this author, would emphasize that working with older adults has tremendous rewards. It is a professional and personal joy to work with older adults who have lived through the most interesting of times and delight in retelling their life stories. Seeing the power of the human spirit in older adults who have survived and thrived through raising families, struggling with careers inside and outside the home, and reframing the meaning and purpose of their lives during the later years is a very positive and revitalizing experience for any professional. Older adults can be delightfully humorous, frustratingly stubborn, amazingly persistent, but always the most powerful reminder of the resiliency of the individual to grow and flourish throughout the life span.

SUMMARY

One of the greatest challenges to society and the profession of social work is the dramatic increase in the number of persons over age 65 in the twenty-first century. Although the baby boomer generation will no doubt forge new ways to meet the demands of this developmental stage, quality health care, a productive postretirement lifestyle, and adequate financial resources pose challenges to today's and tomorrow's older adults. For some older women and older adults of color, the devastating effects of a lifetime of poverty and substandard health care will follow them into old age. These groups are the most vulnerable older adults.

The future of gerontological social work is bright not only because of the growing demand for specially trained practitioners but also because of the variety of settings in which social workers will be needed. In addition to traditional settings, such as hospitals and nursing homes, social workers can be found in community settings, legislative offices, and legal settings. These settings will demand a high level of skill in specific practice techniques and a willingness to engage in the self-awareness necessary for professional work with older adults. Working with older adults can trigger powerful feelings about death, the aging of family members, and one's own attitudes about helping this vulnerable population. However, this population is also one of the most rewarding for social workers.

References

Administration on Aging. (2010). *A profile of older Americans, 2010*. Washington, DC: U.S. Department of Health and Human Services.

Assisted Living Federation of America. (2011). *What is assisted living?* Alexandria, VA: Author. Retrieved March 17, 2011, from http://www.alfa.org

Bureau of Labor Statistics (2010). *Labor force statistics from the Current Population Survey*. Retrieved March 17, 2011, from http://www.bls.gov/data/#employment

Butler, R. N. (1989). Dispelling ageism: The cross-cutting intervention. In M. W. Riley & J. W. Riley, Jr. (Eds.), The quality of aging: Strategies for interventions. *Annals of the American Academy of Political and Social Science, 503*, 163–175.

Cahill, K. E., Giandrea, M. D., & Quinn, J. F. (2006). Retirement patterns from career employment. *The Gerontologist, 46*(4), 514–523.

Centers for Disease Control and Prevention and the Merck Company Foundation. (2007). *The state of aging and health in America 2007*. Whitehouse Station, NJ: The Merck Company Foundation, 2007.

DeFrances, C. J., & Podgornik, M. N. (2004). *2004 National hospital discharge survey*. Advance Data from Vital and Health Statistics, p. 371. Washington, DC: U.S. Government Printing Office.

Edelman, P., Guihan, M., Bryant, F. B., & Munroe, D. J. (2006). Measuring resident and family member determinants of satisfaction with assisted living. *The Gerontologist, 46*(5), 599–608.

Fast, B., & Chapin, R. (2000). *Strengths-based care management for older adults*. Baltimore, MD: Health Professions Press.

Federal Interagency Forum on Aging-Related Statistics. (2010). *Older Americans 2010: Key Indicators of Well-Being*. Washington, DC: U.S. Government Printing Office.

Franks, J. (2002). Social workers need to know more about assisted living and vice-versa. *Journal of Social Work in Long-Term Care, 1*(3), 13–15.

Glicken, M. D. (2004). *Using the strengths perspective in social work practice*. Boston, MA: Pearson.

Joslin, K., & Fleming, R. (2001). Case management in the law office. *Journal of Gerontological Social Work, 34*(3), 33–48.

Madden, R. G., & Wayne, R. H. (2003). Social work and the law: A therapeutic jurisprudence perspective. *Social Work, 48*(3), 338–347.

Massachusetts Senior Action. (2011). *Senior action leader* (Vol. 1). Dorchester, MA: Author.

MetLife Mature Market Institute. (2006). *Living longer, working longer: The changing landscape of the aging workforce: A MetLife Study*. New York: MetLife Mature Market Institute, DeLong, D., & Zogby International. Retrieved September 1, 2007, from https://www.metlife.com/assets/cao/mmi-studies-living-longer.pdf

Merrill Lynch. (2005). *The Merrill Lynch new retirement survey*. New York: Author. Retrieved September 1, 2007, from http://www.totalmerrill.com/retirement

Munnell, A. H., Webb, A., & Delorme, L. (2006). *A new rational retirement risk index*. An Issue in Brief: June 2006. Boston, MA: Center for Retirement Research at Boston College. Retrieved September 1, 2007, from http://www.bc.edu/crr

Nathan, J. (2010). The place of psychoanalytic theory and research in reflective social work practice. In M. Webber and J. Nathan (Eds.), *Reflective practice in mental health* (pp. 121–139) Philadelphia, PA: Jessica Kingsley Publishers.

National Academy of Elder Law Attorneys. *Elders and social justice.* Vienna, VA. Retrieved March 17, 2011, from http://www.naela.org.

National Adult Day Services Association. (2011). *Adult day services.* Retrieved March 17, 2011, from http://www.nadsa.org

National Association of Professional Geriatric Care Managers. (2011). *What is a geriatric care manager?* Tucson, AZ: Author. Retrieved March 17, 2011, from http://www.caremanager.org/gcm

National Association of Social Workers. (2011). *PACE: Building political power for social workers.* Washington, DC: Author. Retrieved March 1, 2011, from http://www.naswdc.org/pace

National Center for Health Care Statistics. (2004). *Data from the 1995 National Nursing Home Survey* (PHS 97-1250). Washington, DC: U.S. Government Printing Office.

National Center for Health Care Statistics. (2011). *Health, United States, 2010.* Washington, DC. Retrieved March 1, 2011, from http:cdc.gov/nchs/data/hus/hus10.pdf

National Women's Law Center. (2010). *Poverty among women and families 2000–2009.* Washington, DC. Retrieved March 15, 2012, from http://www.nwlc.org/sites/default/files/povertyamongwomenand-families2009final.pdf

Peck, M. R. (2009). Personal death anxiety and communication about advance directives among oncology social workers. *Journal of Social Work and End-of-Life & Palliative Care, 5*(1), 49-60.

Reidbord, S. (2010). *Countertransference: An overview.* Sacramento Street Psychology. Retrieved March 15, 2012, from http://www.psychologytoday.com/blog/sacramento-street-psychiatry/201003/countertransference-overview

Saleebey, D. (1992). *The strengths perspective in social work practice.* New York: Longman.

Salmon, J. R., Polivka, L., & Soberon-Ferrer, H. (2006). The relative benefits and cost of Medicaid home and community based services in Florida. *The Gerontologist, 46*(4), 483–494.

Sember, B. M. (2008). *The complete guide to senior care.* Naperville, IL: Sphinx.

Stone, R., Reinhard, S. C., Machemer, J., & Rudin, D. (2002). *Geriatric care managers: A profile of an emerging profession.* Washington, DC: AARP Public Policy Institute. Retrieved March 1, 2011, from http://www.aarp.org/health/doctors-hospitals/info-2002/geriatric_care_managers_a_profile_of_an_emerging_profession.html

Taylor, S. (2006). Educating future practitioners of social work and law: Exploring the origins of interprofessional misunderstanding. *Children and Youth Services Review, 28*(6), 638–653.

U.S. Bureau of the Census. (1993). *Population projections of the United States by age, sex, race and Hispanic origin, 1993–2050.* Current Population Reports, P25-1104. Washington, DC: U.S. Government Printing Office.

U.S. Bureau of the Census. (1996). *Population projections of the United States by age, sex, race and Hispanic origin, 1995–2050.* Current Population Reports, P25-1130, 1996; Census data 1900–1990. Table G, Percent Distribution by Age 1990–2050.

Vinton, L. (2004). Perceptions of the need for social work in assisted living facilities. *Journal of Social Work in Long Term Care, 3*(1), 85–100.

Volland, P. J., & Keepnews, D. M. (2006). Generalized and specialized hospitals. In B. Berkman (Ed.), *Handbook of social work in health and aging* (pp. 413–422). New York: Oxford University Press.

Vourlekis, B., & Simons, K. (2006). Nursing homes. In B. Berkman (Ed.), *Handbook of social work in health and aging* (pp. 601–614). New York: Oxford University Press.

Wacker, R. R., & Roberto, K. A. (2008). *Community resources for older adults.* Thousands Oaks, CA: Sage.

Wallace, G. (2001). Grandparent caregivers: Emerging issues in elder law and social work practice. *Journal of Gerontological Social Work, 34*(3), 127–136.

The following questions will test your application and analysis
of the content found within this chapter.

1. Professional supervision is critical to social workers but especially to those working with older adults because

   a. many older clients will die and increase the likelihood of depression for the social worker.

   b. older adults are the most difficult client population to work with.

   c. every social worker will need to confront the reality of his or her own and family members' aging.

   d. there are few solutions to the problems of older adults.

2. A geriatric care manager has been working with an 85-year-old man who is able to live alone but needs housekeeping and home health services. Suddenly, he becomes very hostile and refuses to let the care manager into his home. The first thing the social worker should do is

   a. call Adult Protective Services to force the man to let her in his home.

   b. call the man's physician to get a prescription for antidepressants.

   c. contact a family member to alert him or her to the recent change.

   d. see if one of the neighbors has a key to the man's home.

3. An older adult with many physical and cognitive problems adamantly insists on staying on in her own home despite her family's wishes that she consider an assisted-living facility or a nursing home. The family cannot provide direct assistance but can pay for services. What should the social worker do?

4. A wealthy older woman is facing nursing home placement but her family wants to keep her assets from being spent for her care to protect their inheritance. If she has fewer assets she will be eligible for medical assistance and her care will be free in a nursing home. The family asks you for advice. What should the social worker do?

Biological Changes and the Physical Well-Being of Older Adults

Biological changes associated with the natural aging process are often the first overt signals to adults that they are moving from middle age to becoming an older adult. Although inevitable changes in the body occur in all aging people, the extent to which these changes precipitate chronic illness or impair functioning varies dramatically. Many older adults remain physically active well into their 80s, experiencing only minor inconveniences caused by sight, hearing, or joint changes. Others struggle with debilitating chronic illnesses beginning in their 60s and become increasingly frail in their 70s. These differences are due to a variety of factors, including genetic predisposition to certain physical ailments, general lifetime health status, and most important, the influence of lifestyle choices, including nutrition and exercise. This chapter begins with a discussion of what physical changes associated with aging mean to older adults themselves. While every stage in human development brings significant biological changes, those associated with the aging process often limit people's life choices and functioning rather than enhance them.

This chapter will explore the normal and abnormal biological changes associated with the aging process, including the discussion of theories about why aging occurs and the cellular-level changes that affect all the physiological systems of the human body. Special consideration is given to the problem of urinary incontinence, a life-changing development that challenges the capability for independent living for some older adults. A growing concern for gerontological social workers and health-care providers is the increasing incidence of HIV/AIDS among older adults, which is discussed as well. The chapter concludes with a discussion of the influence of nutrition, fall prevention, and exercise on an older adult's health and well-being, factors that have substantial influence on the quality of physical health for older adults, regardless of genetic predisposition to the development of disease or the natural changes that accompany the aging process.

Competencies Applied with Practice Behaviors Examples —In This Chapter

☑ Professional Identity

☑ Ethical Practice

☐ Critical Thinking

☐ Diversity in Practice

☑ Human Rights & Justice

☐ Research-Based Practice

☐ Human Behavior

☑ Policy Practice

☐ Practice Contexts

☐ Engage, Assess, Intervene, Evaluate

WHAT DO BIOLOGICAL CHANGES MEAN FOR OLDER ADULTS?

Physical Health Becomes an Organizing Principle

For older adults suffering from physical limitations and chronic illness, day-to-day health status becomes the organizing principle in their lives. How they feel physically is the barometer for their willingness to leave their homes, participate in social activities, and interact with others. Some older adults may feel their bodies have become prisons. As much as they might want to be more active, their physical well-being, rather than personal motivation, dictates what is possible. Consequently, older adults may be evasive about committing to participation in future activities. Although willing, they may feel it is more practical to say, "Well, I'll see how I feel on that day." Older adults with chronic health problems may experience good days and bad days, so it is true that how they feel on any given day determines what they can or cannot do. This hesitancy to make firm plans should not be interpreted as resistance but rather as a very practical way to handle the uncertainties of fragile health. This can be a source of endless frustration for the social worker in trying to facilitate involving an older adult in activities outside the home.

However, even significant chronic health conditions do not mean older adults have to completely withdraw from interaction with others. Too many older adults simply assume that nothing can be done about the aches and pains they associate with aging. They may resolve themselves to suffer silently. The aging process should not be synonymous with pain. The strengths perspective proposes that older adults can find physical and social activities that are geared to the remaining abilities and the benefits from adaptive activities far outweigh the risks. For example, an adaptive yoga program can actually help minimize arthritis pain rather than exacerbate it. An amplification device in a movie theater will help an older adult with a significant hearing loss enjoy a movie along with friends or family. The social worker's role is twofold: to help older adults identify the physical abilities they have *not* lost and to encourage older adults to remain connected to enjoyable activities by facilitating adaptation when necessary. For older adults, physical health will continue to be an organizing principle in their lives but there are a host of possibilities for working with and around health limitations.

An important premise of gerontological social work is that older adults have the right to maximum physical and emotional comfort whenever possible. It is paramount that social workers encourage older adults to seek medical attention when they experience pain and to be assertive when dealing with their physicians. Social workers can play an important role in empowering older adults to help physicians and other health-care providers to be more responsive to their needs.

Abilities and Attitudes Are at Odds

One of the most common reactions social workers hear from older adults as they face the changes that accompany the biological changes of aging is how much younger older adults feel in their minds than their aging bodies would suggest. They are acutely aware of (and infinitely frustrated by) the sense that chronic health problems are a form of betrayal by their bodies. Older adults may experience a form of cognitive dissonance in which they feel strangely alienated from their bodies, thus being more likely to underestimate what they can or cannot do. For example, every year an older man may insist on going up on the roof to clear the gutters of leaves and debris even though his balance is compromised or his sight is impaired. What looks like a foolish move by his family may be the man's assertion that he always has been able to do this chore and will continue to do it. He is proving something to himself and others. An older woman's refusal to use a cane, even though she is unsteady on her feet, may be a combination of denial of her physical limitations and a fear of being seen as "old" by others. While family members may describe aging relatives as stubborn, it is likely due to a much more complex process.

This process also may limit older adults from continuing to engage in activities because they underestimate what they still can do. An underlying premise of the strengths perspective is that even the most seriously compromised older adult is still capable of engaging in some level of self-care or enjoyable activity. Even with serious sight limitations, an avid reader can use "talking books" to continue the connection to reading. A lifelong runner who develops arthritis may need to substitute walking for running but it still means vigorous physical exercise. Perhaps an older adult with Alzheimer's disease can no longer play the piano but he or she can listen to music. Finding a way to keep older adults connected to activities and others is a major goal of social work with older adults.

Private Functions Become Public Business

Discussing physical health problems with a social worker or even health-care providers may be particularly uncomfortable for older adults. For an older woman who has been very modest about personal matters such as bladder and bowel functions, discussing these topics with a relative stranger may be awkward. The same is true for an older man who does not feel his difficulties with maintaining an erection or urinating are anyone's business. What have been private functions for older adults all their lives tend to become public business when helping professionals get involved. Although a solid understanding of an older adult's health problems is essential to the development of an intervention plan, it is important to be sensitive to the deeply personal nature of this discussion.

Not only do helping professions bring very personal business into part of many discussions, so do older adults both individually and in a group setting. The social worker may be very uncomfortable when an older adult focuses on physical problems as the major concern rather than identifying loneliness or depression, issues the social worker feels better prepared to address. It does not take long in a group setting of older adults for the issue of health to emerge as a major topic because it has such a profound effect on older adults' lives. If it is true that "misery loves company," it is easy for group social activities to remain fixated on common health problems. It is important for older adults to feel they can express their concerns but it can also become a barrier to older adults' mobilizing other strengths they can use to improve the quality of their lives.

Environmental Adaptation Is Necessary

With a strong knowledge base in the physical changes associated with aging, social workers can be helpful to institutions and families in designing environmental adaptations to accommodate these changes, part of the effort toward developing *elder friendly*

*Strength-based — make them focus on the positives — Help ∩'s find what they still have. <u>NOT</u> what they have lost.

communities. Handrails can help the unsteady older adult manage stairs or negotiate hallways. Using bright colors to distinguish individual steps and nonglare surfaces on floors can help the sight-impaired older adult avoid falls. Large-print signs and color-coded doors can help older adults reorient themselves in unfamiliar environments. Avoiding background music in senior centers and nursing homes helps older adults concentrate on conversations without having to filter out distracting noises. Anticipating the kinds of environmental changes necessary for older adults with sensory and physical limitations can be helpful in avoiding accidents and making older adults feel more confident in both home and public settings.

WHY DOES THE BODY AGE?

Before looking at the biological changes that accompany the aging process, it is important to explore why scientists believe biological aging occurs. If the cause of aging can be scientifically determined, can the process be stopped? Would it be desirable to significantly lengthen people's lives? These are some social questions that derive from the interest in knowing why the human body ages. The biological questions center more on ways to slow the process of aging. This includes minimizing the development of disease and improving the quality of life for older adults as their bodies grow older. The scientific community does not agree on what initiates the biological aging process, but the primary theories currently espoused fall into three categories: genetic programming, cross-linked cells and free radicals, and changes in the immunological system. These categories do not exhaust all current theories of aging but represent the major areas of scientific inquiry under serious scrutiny.

Genetic Programming

Proponents of the "wear-and-tear" theory of aging suggest that the body simply wears out, reflecting a preprogrammed process determined by genetic makeup. Under this theory, the human body has a maximum life span, and major physiological systems deteriorate at a relatively set rate (Finch, 1991; Hayflick, 1994; McCormick & Campisi, 1991). Cells are programmed with a finite number of divisions, the process that creates new cells and replaces damaged cells (Harvard Gazette Archives, 2001). This deterioration is hastened by environmental and lifestyle factors, but is genetically predetermined. The development of age-related diseases, such as glaucoma, Alzheimer's disease, and late-onset diabetes, may be determined by genetic markers. Genetic markers for certain diseases would explain why certain conditions run in families. There is strong evidence that longevity (without disease) runs in families by a combination of sheer genetic luck and healthy living. However, the genetic programming theory of aging is not universally accepted as the only explanation of the biological changes associated with aging.

Cross-Links and Free Radicals

Cellular biologists propose that aging begins with adverse reactions within the structure of cells and molecules, but those changes are not necessarily initiated by a genetic program. According to this theory, molecules in the body develop cross-links within themselves and with other molecules that create subtle changes in the physical and chemical functioning of the cell (Aldwin & Gilmer, 2004). Cells accumulate collagen, a gelatinous substance present in connective tissues, which reduces the elasticity of tissue. The accumulation occurs because the body is not efficient in recognizing and eliminating cross-linked cells. This accumulation is observable in cartilage, blood vessel, and skin cells (Grune & Davies, 2001). Cartilage becomes less flexible, leading to the joint stiffness associated with aging; blood vessels harden, and skin wrinkles.

Another molecular-level explanation for aging is the free radical theory (Grune & Davies, 2001). Free radicals are unstable oxygen molecules produced when cells metabolize oxygen. These molecules attach to proteins in the body, impairing the functioning of healthy cells. The damage to the body occurs when cross-links and free radicals accumulate, damaging cellular structures. Free radicals are believed to impair the body's ability to fight cancer, repair skin cell damage, and prevent low-density fat cells from clinging to artery walls. Adding antioxidants to multivitamins represents an effort to stabilize free radicals and thus slow the process of cell damage and promote healing. (See Figure 2.1 for more information on antioxidants.)

Deterioration of the Immune System

The body's immune system is responsible for fighting disease and ridding the body of foreign substances. To accomplish that function, the immune system produces antibodies that attack viruses, bacteria, and aberrant cells, such as those produced by cancer. The immunological theory of aging proposes that the immune system's ability to recognize and fight disease is compromised with age (Effros, 2001). Abnormal cells are more likely to grow unchecked, causing chronic disease states that eventually lead to impaired functioning in major physiological systems. Other theories within this school of thought propose that immunological inefficiency results in an autoimmune response by the body. The body slowly rejects its own cells and produces antibodies that destroy even normal cells.

Figure 2.1 • What Are Antioxidants?

Antioxidants are vitamins and nutrients that have been identified as substances with chemical properties that stabilize free radical oxygen cells, thus slowing the damaging effects of deterioration on the cellular level. The three most common antioxidants are beta carotene, Vitamin C, and Vitamin E, all of which occur abundantly in familiar fruits and vegetables.

Antioxidant	Food Sources
Beta carotene	Yellow, orange, and red vegetables and fruit (such as squash, carrots, pumpkins, kale, spinach, peaches, oranges, and tomatoes)
Vitamin C	Citrus fruits, strawberries, cantaloupe, pineapple, brussels sprouts, tomatoes, spinach, kale, cabbage, and turnips
Vitamin E	Vegetable oil, wheat germ, whole grains, and nuts

Source: Reprinted from the International Food Information Council Foundation, 2006.

Arthritis and diabetes are given as examples of the body's autoimmune reaction (Effros, 2001).

None of these theories is accepted as the "true" cause of aging in the human body, but each approach offers some future promise for understanding what happens in the process. All three theories suggest that the process of aging begins on the cellular level, and those changes accumulate throughout a person's lifetime, resulting in the physical changes observed in older adults. Later in the chapter, the influence of noncellular levels, such as nutrition, diet, and the environment, will be discussed. The next section of this chapter explores specifically what changes accompany the process of normal aging and identifies what disease states may develop in each of the major physiological systems of the body.

BIOLOGICAL CHANGES THAT ACCOMPANY AGING

The material presented in the rest of this chapter is offered as the "bio" part of the biopsychosocial approach to assessing older adults and identifying interventions. This material is presented early in the text because an older adult's health and physical well-being are significant indicators of the type of services an older adult will need to function as independently as possible. A basic knowledge about biology does not substitute for a medical assessment by a physician, and social workers should never assume the role of a medical expert. A change in mental status, frequent falls, the presence of pain, dizziness, or the sudden loss of any functional ability should be red flags to the older adult and his or her family that immediate medical attention is needed.

The normal process of biological changes in the human body over time is known as senescence. Aging of the physical body is not considered pathology, nor is normal aging considered a disease. Certain biological changes that occur during this life stage may predispose older adults to the development of illness and disease. However, physical changes in the human body that occur during senescence do not necessarily portend poor health. This section of the chapter will explore the kinds of biological changes that define aging in all the major physiological systems. Individual bodies actually age at different rates, and changes in physiological systems can vary within an individual. However, the process of physical changes that denote aging follows an observable pattern.

Skin, Hair, and Nails

The dermatological system of the body includes the skin, hair, and nails. The most obvious physical change that accompanies the aging process is wrinkling of the skin, caused by a loss of subcutaneous fat and water beneath the skin's surface. This process is compounded by the loss of the elastic fibers within skin cells. Skin becomes thinner and less flexible as the body ages (Spirduso, 1995). Sun exposure is also the primary cause of intense pigmentation on the hands and face, known as liver spots. Ethnicity, lifetime skin care, and physical health contribute to the rate at which these changes in the skin occur. Persons who have had excessive exposure to the sun may begin to show wrinkling of the skin as early as the 30s. African-American older adults, on the contrary, may be well into their 50s and 60s before any wrinkling occurs. This is due to a difference in oil content in their skin.

Between the ages of 30 and 70, the process in which skin cells are replaced as a normal part of the body's maintenance process slows by 50 percent (Tabloski, 2010). Skin is more delicate in older adults, and replacing damaged skin cells occurs more slowly. This combination explains why older adults bruise more easily than younger adults. Bumps and falls may result in much more severe bruising than would seem warranted from the injury, especially for the very old. Blood circulation to the skin's surface slows as the body ages as part of a general decline in the efficiency of the circulatory system and contributes to a slower healing process when skin is injured. Older adults need 50 percent more time to heal from wounds than younger persons (Aldwin & Gilmer, 2004).

Impaired blood circulation to the skin's surface is often responsible for older adults' sensitivity to both cold and heat. Older adults are less likely to shiver to generate body heat or to sweat to dissipate body heat. As a result, aging bodies are less efficient at regulating body temperature in general. Rooms may need to be three to five degrees warmer for older adults to feel comfortable (Hooyman & Kiyak, 2002). The potential problem created by an older adult's inability to regulate body temperature properly is a serious issue. Hypothermia, low body temperature caused by prolonged exposure to the cold, can eventually lead to stroke, brain damage, and death. Hyperthermia, high body temperature caused by prolonged exposure to excessive heat, can cause heat stroke, which if left untreated can be fatal. Therefore, weather variations of both hot and cold are particularly dangerous for older adults, who may experience the effects of extreme temperatures long before younger persons (Tabloski, 2010). When older adults fail to use fans or air conditioning in the summer or keep their thermostats turned low in the winter to save energy costs, they place themselves in physical danger.

Graying of the hair is another common feature of normal aging, although for some individuals this process commences long before old age. Graying occurs when hair follicles lose melanin, the pigment present in hair and skin. This process occurs gradually so that some older adults are completely white haired, whereas others retain varying amounts of their natural hair color throughout life. Hair becomes thinner, beginning in the 40s, due to the body's decreased production of estrogen and testosterone combined with the scalp's decreased efficiency in replacing lost hair. Men may become partially bald, a phenomenon more determined by genetic factors than the aging process. While hair on the head becomes thinner, hair growth may actually increase on other parts of the body in both men and women. Greater hair growth in the nose, ears, and eyebrows suggests that these hormonal deficiencies affect parts of the body in different ways (Hayflick, 1994).

As the body ages, nails become thicker, often turning yellow or gray. Fungal infections of the finger and toenails become more common as evidenced by thick, discolored nails that protrude from the nail bed (Tabloski, 2010). Although these fungal infections are not life-threatening, they can make wearing shoes uncomfortable and/or limit an older adult's mobility. As joints stiffen, older adults often have trouble taking care of toenails, in particular, leading to other foot problems caused by ingrown nails, bacterial infections, and poor circulation due to arthritis or diabetes (National Institute on Aging, 2000).

The Neurological System

The changes in the neurological system associated with normal aging affect all the other physiological systems in the human body. The neurological system consists of the brain and the supporting network of nerves in the body. Although brain weight is reduced by

10 percent by age 75 due to loss of fluid, this change in itself does not cause a loss of brain functioning (Young, 2001). The human brain has a phenomenal capacity to compensate for changes in its physical structure by rerouting functions to different parts of the brain, particularly those that control intelligence and cognitive operations. The actual amount of brain damage due to organic disorders or injuries cannot always predict what, if any, functions will be affected.

The most notable changes associated with aging come from a decline in the efficiency of neurotransmitters, the chemicals that transmit signals within the brain and from the brain to corresponding parts of the body. The synapses, the points at which electrical impulses pass between nerve cells, conduct impulses more slowly as the body ages (Hill-O'Neill & Shaughnessy, 2002). It takes a longer time for the neurological system to send a message to the brain, process a response, and return the message. That is why older adults may have a longer reaction time to certain stimuli (Aldwin & Gilmer, 2004). For example, if an older adult touches a hot surface, he or she may take longer to process the brain's message to remove a hand from the source of heat. Or, while driving, older adults may take longer to react to a car darting into traffic or to the need to stop suddenly. An older adult's cognitive functioning may be intact but require just moments longer to retrieve and process knowledge. The decreased efficiency of the neurological system is in part responsible for problems with hypo- and hyperthermia discussed earlier.

Changes in sleep patterns are considered part of the neurological changes associated with normal aging. Older adults experience less "efficient" sleep, meaning they spend less time in the deeper stages of restorative sleep and feel less rested when they wake up. This is due to changes in brain wave activity and changes in circadian rhythms, the normal pattern of sleep and waking (Eliopoulos, 2005). A younger adult usually sleeps for 7 or 8 hours and is awake for the remaining 16 hours of the day. Older adults may need only 6 hours of sleep but fall into a pattern of napping during the day, a circadian rhythm that more closely resembles an infant's pattern rather than that of an adult. That is why it is common for older adults to go to bed very early but be wide awake in the middle of the night. When older adults nap during the day to compensate for fatigue or use sleeping aids to promote longer nighttime sleep, the problem is compounded. A later bedtime may help older adults to stabilize their own circadian rhythms and restore better-quality sleep.

Two sleep disorders deserve mention in the discussion about neurological disorders. Sleep apnea, the cessation of breathing during sleep for 10 to 15 seconds, can cause insufficient blood flow to the heart. Over time, this can contribute to or exacerbate heart disease. This condition is often treated by raising the head of an older adult's bed or by using plastic breathing strips (the kind used by professional athletes) to open nasal airways. Other older adults experience nocturnal myoclonus, a neurological disorder characterized by involuntary leg jerking in one's sleep (Hayflick, 1994). Although this is not a serious condition, it often disrupts sleep.

Stroke and Parkinson's disease are two other conditions that are found disproportionately in older adults. A stroke is caused by a lack of blood flow to the brain due to clotting or bleeding in the brain as a result of a damaged blood vessel. Eighty-five percent of all cerebrovascular disease occurs in persons over the age of 65 (Young, 2001). Although some strokes are fatal, others leave older adults with seriously diminished physical, cognitive, or communicative abilities. Most strokes are preceded by a series of <u>transient ischemic</u> <u>attacks (TIAs)</u>, which are actually ministrokes. During a TIA, the person experiences a short-term loss of speech, weakness on one side of the body, altered vision, or memory loss (Hill-O'Neill & Shaughnessy, 2002). The impairment lasts only a short time, and the individual usually recovers these lost functions promptly. However, TIAs are warnings of an impending stroke. Transient ischemic attacks can be treated, thus avoiding a stroke and its devastating damage. <u>Parkinson's disease</u> is a second serious neurological disease diagnosed more commonly in older adults than younger persons. <u>Parkinson's disease</u> is a movement disorder characterized by tremors of the fingers, feet, lips, and head with progressive rigidity of the facial and trunk muscles (Young, 2001). Older adults with the disease may have difficulty swallowing or might shuffle when they walk because of attenuated ability to control their extremities. If detected early, the disease responds well to medication.

The Cardiovascular System

The cardiovascular system, the heart and blood vessels, becomes less efficient as the body ages. Increased amounts of fat and collagen are deposited in the heart muscles, reducing cardiac output (Aldwin & Gilmer, 2004). The valves of the heart become more rigid, making the heart work harder. This restricted blood flow accounts for why older adults may tire more easily when doing physical activities or have reduced muscle strength. When older adults most need more efficient circulation, their bodies are less able to provide it for them.

All major blood vessels have some degree of <u>atherosclerosis</u>, deposits of fat that accumulate over a lifetime. These deposits make it more difficult for the heart to pump the blood efficiently throughout the body and to use oxygen efficiently (Young, 2001). These fatty deposits reduce the size and elasticity of the large arteries that pump blood to large organs, such as the stomach, liver, and brain. With reduced blood flow, these organs function less effectively. The cardiovascular system, more than any other system in the human body, can be improved by exercise. Even a minimal amount of exercise by older adults can improve cardiovascular functioning. For older adults who have been athletic throughout their lives, the heart can continue to function as efficiently as that of a much younger person. Although the propensity to develop heart disease is strongly affected by genetic and lifestyle factors, exercise is an equally important determinant of how well the heart ages (American Heart Association, 2011).

Two primary types of cardiovascular disease contribute to making heart disease the number one killer of older adults (American Heart Association, 2011). The first is coronary artery disease, which develops in the form of arteriosclerosis, hardening of the arteries, or atherosclerosis. Coronary heart disease can restrict blood flow to the heart, resulting in heart muscle damage known as a myocardial infarction or a heart attack. Older adults have more diffuse symptoms of a heart attack than younger persons and complain more about a generalized discomfort and fatigue rather than an intense, heavy pain in the chest. Congestive heart failure occurs when the heart fails to pump enough blood throughout the body. Older adults may complain about chronic fatigue, weakness, or edema, the accumulation of fluid in the joints. The discomfort associated with edema often causes older adults to become sedentary, further exacerbating the circulation problem and making older adults prone to other conditions such as pneumonia. Some older adults with chronic heart disease develop cardiac cachexia or "cardiac wasting," a condition characterized by rapid and continuous weight loss accompanied by deterioration of muscle tissue (Strassburg, Springer, & Anker, 2005). These older adults become dangerously thin as their muscles atrophy from insufficient blood flow from a poorly functioning heart.

A second serious cardiovascular disease, not restricted to the older adults, is hypertension or high blood pressure. Hypertension is twice as common among African-American older adults as it is among their white counterparts (Aldwin & Gilmer, 2004). High blood pressure has no symptoms and is often referred to as "the silent killer," although it is easily diagnosed through simple blood pressure screening. High blood pressure damages the arteries, predisposing people to the development of a blood clot, which is a common cause of stroke. It can be treated effectively with medication if the medication is taken consistently and the condition is diagnosed before the hypertension causes extensive damage to the arterial system (Young, 2001).

The Musculoskeletal System

As people grow older, they actually become shorter due to the compression of the vertebrae in the spine. Although both men and women lose some body height, women may become up to three inches shorter due to skeletal changes associated with the loss of estrogen following menopause (Tabloski, 2010). The spine may become more curved, contributing to the illusion that older adults are chronically slouching. Aging is accompanied by a general loss of muscle strength and endurance due to atrophy of muscle cells, loss of lean muscle mass, and loss of elastic fibers in the muscle tissue. The combination of a curved spine and loss of muscle strength contributes to a tendency for older adults to have difficulties in maintaining their balance. They may have a decreased ability to orient their bodies by making subtle changes in the muscles that help them center their bodies over their feet. If older adults feel less stable on their feet, they are likely to move more slowly to maintain control over balance. Some older adults limit physical activity in general, which accelerates the deterioration of muscle strength and coordination.

The teeth and supporting jaw structure, considered part of the musculoskeletal system, may or may not deteriorate as an individual ages. Older adults who have not had access to lifetime preventative dental care or fluorinated water are usually at greater risk for losing their teeth prior to or during their later years. The most common cause of tooth loss for persons over the age of 65 years is periodontal disease, infections of the gums and bone structure of the jaw that hold teeth in place (Administration on Aging, 1999). These infections are usually caused by dental plaque, which can be removed with regular brushing and routine cleaning of the teeth. Once older adults have lost their natural teeth and wear dentures, the structure of the jaw may change. Dentures may no longer fit, and the mouth may actually shrink. When dentures fit poorly, older adults tend to avoid wearing them, hastening the process of shrinkage. This cyclical process may make chewing very difficult and even painful.

The most common musculoskeletal disease associated with aging is arthritis, which is estimated to affect between 43 and 60 million Americans (Arthritis Foundation, 2007). It is rare for persons over the age of 75 not to have at least some minor osteoarthritis in joints. This condition is caused by deterioration of cartilage accompanied by the development of bone spurs on the joint surface (Aldwin & Gilmer, 2004). Deterioration of cartilage occurs naturally as the result of a lifetime of using joints or as a consequence of joint injury. Although arthritis can be extremely painful, the most damaging consequence of the disease is its debilitating effect on an older adult's mobility. Older adults may avoid social participation because of the difficulty of moving, thus leading to increased social isolation (Militades & Kaye, 2006). It may be painful for older adults to move their hands or knees thus making them far less active; however, regular exercise of arthritic joints can actually improve the condition (Arthritis Foundation, 2007). A more severe form of arthritis, rheumatoid arthritis, is not associated with aging but rather is an autoimmune disease affecting persons of all ages.

Women face one of the most damaging effects of aging on the musculoskeletal system—osteoporosis, the thinning and deterioration of bone integrity. Postmenopausal osteoporosis affects women and is caused by the lack of estrogen in the body following menopause. Not all women will develop osteoporosis. Figure 2.2 describes the personal characteristics that predispose women to the development of the condition.

Senile osteoporosis, which affects both men and women, is defined as the general deterioration of bone density associated with very advanced age. Hip and wrist fractures are more likely when bones are thin and brittle. Although it is often assumed that an older adult's hip breaks as a result of a fall, more recent research indicates that a hip can spontaneously fracture, causing the fall (Baum, Capezuti, & Driscoll, 2002). Some women develop kyphosis, a hump on the spine, also known as "dowager's hump." Others develop deformities of the vertebrae known as scoliosis. These conditions may be painful and severely limit mobility. Once these conditions develop in older adults, modern medicine can do little to reverse them. However, calcium supplements and regular exercise for

---

Figure 2.2 • Osteoporosis: Are You at Risk?

High-Risk Factors That Are Genetically Determined
- Being female
- Having a history of osteoporosis
- Being of Northern European or Asian ancestry
- Being small-boned or very thin
- Having fair coloring, such as blonde or red hair and fair skin
- Inability to digest milk or milk products

Other High-Risk Lifestyle or Medical Factors
- Having had a pregnancy during teen years
- A medical history that includes loss of the ovaries
- Long periods of immobilization due to disease or injury
- Eating disorders, chronic diarrhea, and kidney or liver disease
- Lack of exercise or excessive exercise
- High alcohol intake, low-calcium diets, or a Vitamin D deficiency
- High caffeine intake and smoking

Source: Centers for Disease Control and Prevention, 2007.

postmenopausal women can help stabilize bone loss and are the best preventative measures (National Center for Biotechnology Information, 2010).

The Gastrointestinal System

The gastrointestinal system of the human body includes the esophagus, stomach, liver, and small and large intestines. Some people begin to experience the symptoms of an aging digestive system early in middle age, and other older adults notice little difference other than some diminished appetite due more to sensory losses in taste and smell than to actual changes in the digestive system. A loss of teeth or skeletal changes in the shape and strength of the jaw may contribute to difficulties in chewing, the first step in the long process of digestion. Food that is poorly chewed is more difficult for the entire digestive system to process. As the body ages, the esophagus, the digestive tube going from the mouth to the stomach, may narrow or become less elastic (Eliopoulos, 2005). As a result, it may take more time for food to pass into the stomach. It is common for older adults to feel "full" after eating only a small amount. The stomach secretes fewer digestive juices so that older adults may experience chronic inflammation of the stomach, known as atrophic gastritis (Aldwin & Gilmer, 2004). The symptoms may be as benign as occasional heartburn or as serious as the development of gastric ulcers. The small and large intestines decrease in weight due to the general loss of water in the body that accompanies age. This may be one of the contributing factors to more frequent constipation among older adults.

Serious weight loss may become a problem for older adults who have little appetite or experience digestive problems (Tabloski, 2010). They are less likely to eat if the process of digestion and elimination is uncomfortable. Poor dietary habits, smoking, and genetic predisposition are contributing factors in the higher incidence of stomach and colon cancer among older adults. Both of these types of cancer can be detected and treated early in the progression of the disease, but the key is early detection (Militades & Kaye, 2006). Older adults and their physicians may be more hesitant to undergo an endoscopy, the internal examination of the esophagus and stomach, or a colonoscopy, the internal examination of the colon, out of either fear or ignorance.

The Respiratory System

As in the heart, the exact progression of aging in the respiratory system is the function of a lifetime of both lifestyle and environmental factors. In fact, it is difficult to distinguish between those changes in the respiratory system that are due to pollutants and toxins and those due to the normal process of aging. In general, the muscles that operate the lungs lose elasticity and strength. The loss of strength impairs older adults' ability to breathe deeply, cough, and clear the lungs of mucus and fluids. The number of *cilia*, the hairlike structures in the lungs, are reduced, making lungs less efficient in obtaining oxygen (Tockman, 1995). As the body ages, the lungs have decreased functional reserve capacity, resulting in much slower, shallower breathing (Aldwin & Gelmer, 2004). Less-efficient breathing may result in insufficient oxygen intake for the rest of the body.

Although these changes are quite dramatic, if other lung disease is not present, older adults may experience normal breathing while at rest. It is when their bodies demand more oxygen during activity that the changes become most apparent. Given the opportunity to rest during activity or to perform physical tasks at a slower rate, older adults may function with no apparent dysfunction of the respiratory system.

Chronic oxygen insufficiency, however, can impair the function of the circulatory system and damage the heart. The inability to cough properly to expel foreign matter from the lungs can result in a greater tendency among older adults to develop emphysema, chronic bronchitis, or pneumonia (Tockman, 1995). Pneumonia is the fifth leading cause of death among older adults (Centers for Disease Control and Prevention & The Merck Company Foundation, 2007). Many of the diseases of the lung that develop among older adults are the result of cigarette smoking or environmental pollution.

The Urinary Tract System

For some older adults, the changes in the urinary system, comprised of the kidneys, ureters, and the bladder, are the most bothersome. The kidneys serve two primary functions in the body. Kidneys filter water and waste material from the blood and dispel those wastes in the form of urine. The kidneys also are crucial in restoring the balance of ions and minerals to the filtered blood before it is returned to the bloodstream. The ability of the kidneys to perform both of these functions diminishes by as much as 50 percent as the body ages (Eliopoulos, 2005; Hooyman & Kiyak, 2002). Certain drugs, including antibiotics, become more potent in an older adult's system because less of the drug is naturally filtered out by the kidneys. Kidneys may lose the ability to absorb glucose, thereby contributing to a greater tendency among older adults to become seriously dehydrated.

Both the ureters, the tubes leading from the kidneys to the bladder, and the bladder tend to lose muscle tone, which may result in incomplete emptying of the bladder. When the bladder is not emptied during urination, older adults are more likely to suffer from urinary tract infections. Urinary tract infections are often asymptomatic in older adults and therefore not diagnosed appropriately leading to other serious health issues, such as delirium which is discussed in Chapter 5. Older adults may need to urinate more frequently, due to diminished bladder capacity. This is most likely to occur during the night and may disrupt sleep (Tabloski, 2010). Despite frequency of urination, older adults may experience a delayed sensation of needing to empty the bladder due, in part, to the less efficient operation of the body's neurological system. Incontinence may be the result of this combination of decreased bladder capacity and delayed sensation of urge. The problem, which is discussed in more detail later in this chapter, is more prevalent in women as a result of the relaxation of the lower pelvic muscles following childbirth.

For men, urinary tract problems may be exacerbated by problems associated with the prostate, a doughnut-shaped gland that encircles the urethra and produces most of the fluid in semen. Enlargement of the prostate may result in problems with starting and stopping urine flow, incomplete bladder emptying, or frequent urges to urinate (Aldwin & Gilmer, 2004). Prostate enlargement is not necessarily considered a disease unless the urinary tract system backs up and causes an infection or the prostate becomes cancerous. The risk of developing cancer of the prostate increases with advanced age and a family history of the disease.

The Endocrine and Reproductive Systems

The human body functions on the basis of a complex, carefully regulated system of hormones produced by the endocrine system. Hormones regulate reproduction, growth, energy production, and the general homeostatic condition of the body. The two primary hormonal changes that occur in aging that will be discussed in this section are changes in insulin levels regulated by the pancreas and the reduction of estrogen and testosterone levels in both men and women.

Insulin is produced by the pancreas to regulate glucose levels in the bloodstream. Glucose is one of the sugars in food that is metabolized to produce energy. For some older adults, the pancreatic production of insulin becomes less efficient, and glucose is not metabolized. As a result, blood sugar levels become elevated. Adult-onset diabetes may develop when the body's insulin levels are chronically insufficient. Older adults may not exhibit the usual symptom of fatigue, increased appetite, weakness, slow healing, and frequent urination associated with diabetes. Diabetes may not even be detected in older adults until found in blood tests conducted for other medical reasons. Untreated diabetes leads to frequent infections, kidney failure, and heart and blood vessel damage. Older African-American and Hispanic women are particularly susceptible to diabetes due, in part, to what appears to be a genetic tendency combined with poor diet, physical inactivity, and a greater prevalence of other age-related disease (Tabloski, 2010).

The universal change in the endocrine system for women occurs following menopause, the cessation of the menstrual cycle, which occurs for most women in the late 40s and 50s. As the ovaries cease to function, they reduce the production of estrogen and progesterone. The protective function of estrogen helps to explain why women are at lower risk for heart disease than men until their 50s when the incidence evens out.

Estrogen loss combined with other normal biological changes associated with aging leads to some degree of urogenital atrophy in women (Tabloski, 2010). That is, the vaginal walls become thinner and drier, which may cause pain for women during sexual intercourse. This discomfort can be alleviated with artificial lubricants and should not be interpreted as a woman's inability to enjoy sex.

The normal reproductive changes that occur in aging men happen more gradually than those observed in women. Menopause in women is an observable series of events resulting in loss of reproductive capacity, whereas men may continue their reproductive abilities well into old age. Men may experience some reduction in testosterone levels, which diminishes sex drive, but this is not a universal phenomenon. Men require more direct stimulation and more time as they age to achieve an erection. There is usually a longer refractory period between erections as well. However, men's sexual desire and performance are more likely to be affected by the presence of prostate problems and other health problems than by hormonal insufficiency (Styrcula, 2001).

The Sensory System

All of the sensory systems show some change by age 70. Most older adults lose some sensory acuity in their sight, hearing, taste, and smell and develop a higher sensory threshold in their sense of touch. In the absence of disease, these changes occur gradually, and most older adults learn to compensate for losses.

Touch

Due to the diminished efficiency of neurotransmitters discussed earlier in this chapter, most older adults appear to have a higher threshold for pain or at least a different experience of feeling pain (Timaris, 1988). However, it can be easily disputed that an older adult's experience of pain is simply different than that of younger persons and may routinely be poorly diagnosed (Tabloski, 2010). Pain from serious conditions such as heart attacks may be experienced as a chronic but vague discomfort rather than the intense crushing pain experienced by younger persons (Legato, 1997). Older adults may be less likely to complain about pain from burns or skin lesions, which are even more serious for older adults in view of delayed healing. This loss of sensory threshold can also result in what appears to be increased clumsiness. Older adults may not be able to feel the fine distinctions needed to grasp objects firmly. They may have more difficulty establishing their sense of balance because the neurological system takes longer to send messages to the muscles to work together to maintain balance.

Vision

Changes in vision begin as early as the late 30s, when people begin to experience presbyopia, the inability to change the focus of the lens for near vision. Phone books, newspapers, and other small print become increasingly difficult to read at close range. These changes in sight are due to changes in the shape of the eye. The lens of the eye becomes less elastic and therefore less able to adjust to the rapid change necessary when going from distance vision to close vision. The pupil of the eye is smaller, more fixed, and less responsive to changes in light. As a result, older adults need more light to actually see. The pupil cannot automatically dilate to let in more light. Likewise, the pupil cannot constrict to limit the amount of light coming into the eye, and therefore older adults may have more difficulty when glare from the sun or poor lighting is present. Shiny surfaces, especially floors, present a significant danger to older adults, who are literally blinded by the glare. Older adults may also gradually lose their peripheral vision even if their central vision remains. Sensitivity to glare and a decrease in peripheral vision create very serious problems for some older adult drivers (Stuen, 2006).

The lens of the eye yellows, reducing an older adult's color sensitivity. Blues, violets, and greens become the most difficult to distinguish, although the human eye retains its sensitivity to red, yellow, and orange well into old age (Eliopoulos, 2005). This diminished ability to distinguish between colors contributes to the loss of depth perception and creates an additional risk to older drivers.

Although these changes in vision may be inconvenient and annoying for older adults, they are considered normal age-related changes in vision. A cataract, a film that clouds the lens of the eye, is not part of normal changes in the eye. When cataracts develop, it is often necessary to replace the clouded lens with a removable or permanent contact lens to restore clear vision. Cataracts are found more frequently in African Americans (Stuen, 2006). The development of cataracts is strongly connected to a lack of antioxidants such as vitamins A, C, and E, which are frequently missing in a high-fat, high-carbohydrate diet. A more serious eye condition that frequently leads to blindness is glaucoma, the presence of excessive or insufficient fluid in the eye, which produces abnormal pressure. Untreated, it leads to tunnel vision. Glaucoma is the leading cause of blindness in African Americans. It is easily detected by a simple test given by optometrists and ophthalmologists and can be treated effectively with medication. A third eye disease seen more frequently in older adults than in younger people is macular degeneration, a slow progressive loss of central vision. Older adults with this condition retain some of their peripheral vision but lose the ability to see objects in the direct field of vision.

Hearing

Although normal changes are associated with hearing as the body ages, hearing damage may occur at an early age for some persons. Exposure to loud working environments, such as construction sites, factories, and drilling operations, may cause premature hearing loss as early as the 20s. Another leading cause of non-age-related changes is exposure to loud music at concerts and through personal stereo devices. The ear can repair nerve damage from occasional exposure to damaging sound levels, but constant exposure will result in hearing loss that the body cannot repair. The prevalence of such devices among younger persons suggests that the number of older adults with significant hearing loss in the future will no doubt increase.

The progressive loss of hearing and the inability to distinguish between different frequencies of sound is known as presbycusis. This condition is due to age-related changes in the bones that conduct sound in the inner ear along with loss of cells in the cranial nerve (Gulya, 1995; Hayflick, 1994). Hearing loss may not be so much an issue of whether sounds are loud enough for a person to hear but whether the person is able to distinguish between those sounds. Conversations may sound muffled or jumbled because certain frequencies of the human voice cannot be distinguished. A person with a hearing loss may have decreased ability to filter voices through other background noise. Amplifying the sound may exacerbate the problem. Volume may not be the issue but rather the ability to distinguish between sounds so as to give them meaning. This is especially true of human speech. Some hearing loss is due to a buildup of wax in the ear canal.

Taste and Smell

These two senses are included together because they have such a strong interconnection. The body routinely loses taste buds regardless of age, but even among the very old, these taste buds are regenerated. Despite the replacement of taste buds, however, older adults often report a decreased taste threshold (Aldwin & Gilmer, 2004). Older adults are likely to prefer more highly seasoned foods so that they can taste them or to be attracted to foods that are high in sugar or salt. However, loss of smell may actually be the culprit in older adults' loss of their sense of taste. The number of olfactory receptors diminishes with age despite the process of replacement. Receptors are not replaced at the same rate they are damaged. The inability to smell food decreases the power of taste, therefore diminishing the enjoyment derived from eating. The inability to enjoy food through taste or smell often contributes to a serious loss of appetite among older adults. The inability to smell can be dangerous when older adults do not smell natural gas, smoke and fire, or spoiled food.

Every major physiological system experiences some changes in the aging process, although these changes should not be equated with disease or disability. Some of these changes occur slowly and are hardly noticed by an individual, such as changes in taste or smell. Other changes, such as reduced efficiency of the heart and lungs, present significant challenges to older adults in daily functioning. A summary of the major biological changes associated with the aging process is presented in Table 2.1.

Table 2.1	System Age-Related Biological Changes
Dermatological System (Skin, Hair, Nails)	Skin wrinkles, hair thins and may turn gray. Fingernails and toenails thicken. Older adults may be more susceptible to hyper- or hypothermia. Injuries may take 50 percent longer to heal.
Neurological System (Brain, Nervous System)	Response time to stimuli is slowed. Sleep patterns are less efficient. Older adults are more likely to experience cardiovascular disease with small or major strokes.
Cardiovascular System	Heart may become less efficient if arteriosclerosis or atherosclerosis is present. More likely to have hypertension.
Musculoskeletal System	Older adults may become shorter and lose muscle strength and mass. Arthritis is more likely to develop in joints. Women may develop osteoporosis, resulting in fractures, dowager's hump, or scoliosis.
Respiratory System	Functional capacity of lungs is diminished. Older adults become more easily winded when exerting themselves. May become more susceptible to pneumonia.
Urinary Tract System	Kidneys are less efficient in screening toxins and restoring ionic balance to blood. Bladder loses tone and is more likely to develop asymptomatic infections. Some older adults develop incontinence.
Endocrine/Reproductive System	Some older adults are less efficient at metabolizing glucose and may develop late-onset diabetes. Estrogen loss after menopause may exacerbate osteoporosis.
Sensory System	
Touch	Older adults may develop higher threshold for pain, greater tendency to develop hypo- or hyperthermia. Balance problems may develop.
Vision	Presbyopia is common. Eye needs more light to focus and is sensitive to glare. Older adults may experience reduced ability to distinguish between colors. Some older adults develop cataracts, glaucoma, or macular degeneration.
Hearing	Hearing acuity may be reduced up to 50 percent, with difficulties in distinguishing between sounds.
Taste/Smell	Sense of smell may be seriously impaired due to lifetime environmental damage. Taste is affected by lack of smell. Older adults may not smell gas, smoke, or spoiled food.

INCONTINENCE

One of the significant aspects of physical health in maintaining independent living is the older adult's ability to manage basic bowel and bladder functions with minimal assistance. Urinary incontinence, the involuntary loss of control over the elimination of urine from the body, was once assumed to be an inevitable part of the aging process. The medical community now knows that this is simply not so. The biological changes associated with aging may put older adults at higher risk for the development of incontinence, but the aging process itself is not the cause.

The Prevalence of Incontinence

It is estimated that between 8 and 34 percent of community-dwelling older adults experience incontinence at some time in their lives (Melville, Katon, Delaney, & Newton, 2005; Umlauf & Sherman, 1996). This figure includes approximately one-third of women and one-fifth of men over the age of 65 who are noninstitutionalized (Assad, 2000; Ouslander, 2000). Among older adults residing in nursing homes, this number rises to 50 percent of the population. Health-care providers may not even be aware of the problem among their patients nor initiate a conversation about it with their older adult patients. Umlauf and Sherman (1996) found that less than 25 percent of older adults seen by a physician are asked about incontinence. But it has also been found that less than one-third of older adults who do experience incontinence bring the topic up with their health-care providers (Specht, 2005). The embarrassment of losing bladder control combined with the fear of losing independence and being sent to a nursing home relegates many older adults to suffer in silence. Older adults' concerns about premature institutionalization are legitimate. Incontinence is one of the most frequently cited reasons for long-term institutional placement (Ouslander, 1983; Umlauf & Sherman, 1996). However, if older adults report their incontinence to health-care providers, it may be "managed" by special voiding schedules or protective garments. Even if treatment does not eliminate incontinence, it does substantially improve the quality of life for these older adults (Palmer, 1996; Swenson & Siegal, 1994).

Types of Incontinence

When older adults have experienced many years of incontinence accompanied by serious deterioration of their general health status and/or cognitive functioning, they may suffer from established incontinence. Only 20 percent of incontinence among older adults is considered established incontinence and is primarily due to serious physical pathology, such as advanced muscle deterioration found in advanced cases of Parkinson's disease, multiple sclerosis, or bladder and bowel cancer (Brandeis, Bauman, Hossain, Morris, & Resnick, 1997; Newman & Palmer, 2003). For some older adults with advanced Alzheimer's disease or other organic brain disorders, the cognitive functioning needed to be alert to the need to void and the actual physical act of voiding may not be possible.

A more common form of incontinence is transient incontinence, short-term or temporary loss of bladder control. Women experience incontinence throughout their lives at twice the rate of men due to the unique design of the female urinary tract system and the physiological changes women experience during pregnancy, childbirth, and menopause (Specht, 2005; Swenson & Siegal, 1994). Male problems with incontinence are frequently due to an enlarged or diseased prostate that constricts the urethra and impairs normal bladder functioning. About 80 percent of transient incontinence can be treated, and two-thirds of cases can eventually be cured (Brandeis et al., 1997).

Transient incontinence usually appears as one of four major types. Stress incontinence is characterized by a loss of urine during a sudden activity that increases the pressure on the abdomen or bladder. Sneezing, coughing, laughing, swinging a golf club or tennis racket, and running are activities that may precipitate a loss of urine (Swenson & Siegal, 1994; Tabloski, 2010). It is more common in women than in men and may appear earlier in women's lives than old age. Urge incontinence is described as a sudden and extremely strong need or urge to urinate with little prior warning that the bladder is full. The urge is so strong that individuals may not make it to the toilet in time to void. Losing urine during sleep or after ingesting even small amounts of liquid are common symptoms of urge incontinence. This type of incontinence is often referred to as overactive bladder. Urge incontinence is more common in men than stress incontinence, but women over age 65 tend to suffer from a combination of stress and urge incontinence.

Overflow incontinence occurs when the bladder is full and leaks urine when an individual shifts positions or gets up from a sitting position. When the bladder is not completely emptied upon urination, it fills up quickly, and an older adult may not be aware of the need to void. Diabetes and other diseases may contribute to weak bladder muscles. Bladder stones, tumors, or prostate problems can block the urethra so that the bladder does not empty during normal voiding. The fourth type of transient incontinence is functional incontinence. This form of incontinence is not due to any physiological problems but occurs when an older adult is unable to access toileting facilities when they need to void. Functional incontinence may develop as a result of any impairment in activities of daily living, specifically the ability to transfer, walk, dress, or toilet (Brandeis et al., 1997). Wheelchair-bound older adults may require assistance in getting to and using the toilet. If no caregiver is present to help them, an episode of incontinence may occur. Other older adults may have difficulties communicating the need to void due to damage from a stroke, a movement disorder such as Parkinson's disease, or Alzheimer's disease.

Treatment of Urinary Incontinence

Once the type of incontinence has been identified, health-care providers may recommend one of many different types of treatment (see Table 2.2). The purpose of discussing treatments in this section of the chapter is to educate the social worker to act as an advocate in helping the older adult understand the variety of approaches available to treat incontinence. Knowing what treatment options exist helps the gerontological social worker empower the older adult client to seek treatment rather than live with incontinence as an inevitable condition of aging. Sometimes simple adjustments in lifestyle and behavior can result in an immediate improvement in the condition.

Table 2.2	Summary of Treatment Options for Urinary Incontinence
Type of Incontinence	**Treatment Options**
Stress	Do Kegel exercises
	Practice biofeedback
	Use hormone replacement therapy
	Regulate intake of fluids
	Eliminate caffeine and alcohol
	Wear protective garments
Urge	Check for bladder stones or tumors
	Adjust medication
	Schedule, prompt voiding of bladder
	Improve ability to reach toilet
	Remove obstacles
	Use topical estrogen (women)
Overflow	Obtain medical evaluation for diabetes or spinal cord lesions
	Adjust medications
	Check for fecal impaction
Functional	Adjust medications
	Avoid use of caffeine or alcohol
	Eliminate obstacles to toilet access or provide commode or urinal
	Make clothing easier to remove for toileting
	Address sensory limitations; adjust restraints, if necessary
	Devise signals to caregivers regarding need to void

HIV/AIDS AND OLDER ADULTS

A growing concern among gerontological social workers and health-care providers is the rising number of middle-aged and older adults who are being affected by HIV/AIDS in the United States. Efforts to prevent, diagnose, and treat HIV (human immunodeficiency virus) and AIDS (acquired immune deficiency syndrome) have focused primarily on the younger population in this country since the early 1980s, when the disease was first brought to the attention of the public health community (Crisologo, Campbell, & Forte, 1996; Poindexter & Emlet, 2006). HIV/AIDS threatens all people, regardless of sexual orientation, IV drug use, or age. Persons over the age of 50 account for 10 percent of all new HIV infections in the United States and 28 percent of persons living with HIV/AIDS (Centers for Disease Control and Prevention, 2005b). The fastest-growing source of HIV/AIDS infection for adults over 50 years of age is heterosexual contact (Emlet, 2006a; National Institute on Aging, 2007). Those rates are growing most rapidly among older adults who are African American, Asian/Pacific Islanders, and American Indians/Alaskan Natives.

The "graying" of HIV/AIDS is due in part to the presence of older adults with HIV/AIDS who are surviving into old age after having contracted the disease earlier in life. Advances in treating HIV/AIDS with antiretroviral medicines and preventing the development of secondary infections, such as pneumonia, have allowed persons with HIV/AIDS to live much longer than ever before. However, new infections continue to be diagnosed among adults over the age of 50 and the mortality rates among those newly diagnosed are higher and the survival time after diagnosis is shorter (Emlet & Farkas, 2002).

Why Older Adults May Be More Vulnerable to Contracting HIV/AIDS

Lack of HIV/AIDS Education

Once epidemiologists and public health officials were able to link HIV/AIDS with high-risk behaviors rather than membership in high-risk populations, such as gay males or IV drug users, an aggressive public education program targeted younger populations who were or were likely to become sexually active or exposed to IV drug use (Strombeck & Levy, 1998). Despite the good intentions of HIV/AIDS educators, little focus was placed on the education of older adults outside the gay community. Limited resources, the popular demand for HIV/AIDS education among younger age groups, and a subtle ageist attitude about the unlikelihood of older adults engaging in high-risk behavior all contributed to this oversight and resulted in a lack of knowledge among older adults about HIV/AIDS (Poindexter & Emlet, 2006). Older adults may be at high risk for contracting the disease because many have little, if any, accurate information about high-risk behaviors and are less likely to use condoms (National Association on HIV over Fifty, 2007).

Social Attitudes

A lack of accurate information about HIV/AIDS among older adults has contributed to the social attitude that "it cannot happen to me." Older adults may assume that if they are not having sex with an openly gay or bisexual male or self-professed IV drug user, there is absolutely no way they can contract the disease (National Association on HIV over Fifty, 2007). Older adults may become sexually involved with others they have known for a long time and may make dangerous assumptions about their partners' sexual or drug history. Older adults who are widowed after having been in monogamous relationships for their entire adult lives may not consider that their social acquaintances may have engaged in extramarital affairs or frequented prostitutes in the past.

Biological Vulnerability

Not only are older adults socially more vulnerable to engaging in unprotected sex, thus contracting HIV/AIDS, but the biological changes associated with aging make older adults more vulnerable to contracting the disease. The loss of estrogen in an older woman's body following menopause causes thinning in the vaginal walls (as discussed earlier in this chapter). This thinning makes the vaginal walls more susceptible to small tears, providing a greater opportunity for the virus to enter the body (Bachus, 1998). For those older women utilizing hormone replacement therapy to ease the symptoms of menopause, the additional hormones may actually make them more susceptible to contracting HIV. The hormones estrogen and progestin have been identified as immunodepressive agents that compromise the efficiency of the body's natural immune system. Due to changes in the efficiency of the immune system in the aging body, the presence of HIV has been found to progress more quickly into full-blown AIDS in older adults than in younger persons who contract the disease (Aupperle, 1996; Nokes, 1996). Even without HIV infection, older adults are more likely to develop pneumonia, some cancers, and a range of opportunistic infections. An already compromised immune system deteriorates more quickly in the presence of HIV. Some of the first symptoms of HIV/AIDS are nonspecific and include fatigue, loss of appetite, weight loss, chronic pain, respiratory problems, skin rashes, decreased physical strength, and some loss of cognitive abilities (Poindexter & Emlet, 2006). A health-care provider may consider asking a younger patient presenting with these symptoms about high-risk behaviors and suggest testing for the presence of HIV. However, these same symptoms are common complaints among older adults who may have other chronic conditions, including diabetes, cardiovascular disease, digestive disorders, or even the early stages of dementia (Aupperle, 1996; Bachus, 1998; Strombeck & Levy, 1998). Age-related conditions are more likely to be considered by health-care providers than looking specifically at HIV/AIDS.

HIV/AIDS among Older Adults of Color

African-American males account for 30.8 percent and Hispanic males for 15.1 percent of all cases of HIV/AIDS in the population over 50 years of age. This number is far above their proportional representation in the population (Administration on Aging, 2003; Brown & Sankar, 1998; National Institute on Aging, 2007). The Centers for Disease Control and Prevention (2003) attributed the high rate of HIV/AIDS in these populations to male-to-male sexual contact and disproportionate incidence of IV drug use. These numbers represent a tragic demolition of the older male population of color, a group already compromised by higher mortality rates than their white counterparts. However, two-thirds of new cases of HIV/AIDS in the past 10 years among persons over the age of 50 are women of color, an alarming increase (Centers for Disease Control and Prevention, 2003; National Institute on Aging, 2007). The Centers for Disease Control attributed this increase to greater incidence of unprotected heterosexual sex and the sharing of drug paraphernalia between women of color and persons with HIV/AIDS. Without significant changes in these infection rates, HIV/AIDS may decimate the older population of color.

Socioeconomic Status and Health

Older adults of color are more likely to have low socioeconomic status than their white counterparts. A lifetime of low income contributes to inadequate health care and a greater vulnerability to illness and disease. Chronic health problems combined with the increased susceptibility to diseases that accompany an aging immune system may make the older adult of color particularly vulnerable to contracting HIV/AIDS (Levy-Dweck, 2005). Once an older adult of color is HIV positive, he or she may be less likely to seek treatment for health problems due in part to difficulty in accessing health-care services and a general distrust of the white medical establishment (Brown, 1997).

The Stigma Associated with HIV/AIDS

Despite the alarming numbers of persons of color over age 50 with HIV/AIDS, the condition remains deeply stigmatized in this population (Emlet, 2006b). Among African Americans, homosexuality remains more stigmatized than it is in the white population due to cultural messages about male virility and the cultural influences of traditional black churches that continue to see homosexuality as sinful. The same is true for Hispanic Americans, who fear bringing shame to their families because of the association of HIV/AIDS to male homosexuality. Disclosing one's HIV/AIDS status may be particularly risky in both African-American and Hispanic-American populations as family and friends may reject, rather than support, persons with the disease (Emlet, 2006b).

Implications for Social Work Practice

Improving Preventative Education

Social workers play an important role in arranging and encouraging a comprehensive HIV/AIDS education program aimed at older adults, particularly in areas with a large number of older adults. Senior centers, area agencies on aging, and community health-care centers are excellent venues for educational presentations on HIV/AIDS focused on the needs and interests of older adults. Rose (1996) found that older adults responded most positively to educational programs. Presenting HIV/AIDS education within a climate that stresses how important accurate knowledge is not only encourages safe sex practices among older adults but also helps older adults better understand how the disease affects others, such as adult children, grandchildren, and social acquaintances. Disseminating accurate knowledge about the disease as well as encouraging a compassionate response on the part of older adults to those who are HIV positive are essential parts of the preventative education process (Emlet, 2006b; Levy-Dweck, 2005).

Timely Diagnosis and Treatment

For older adults who have engaged in high-risk behaviors or have a history of blood or organ transfusions, early screening and treatment are imperative. Older adults who are made aware of their own high-risk behaviors are in a better position to work with their health-care providers to consider HIV/AIDS screening as a first line of defense in identifying the cause of health problems rather than as a last resort when all other possible causes have been exhausted. Denial about the possibility of having contracted HIV/AIDS can be a deadly mistake for anyone, but it is even more significant for older adults, whose aging bodies may be less resilient in fighting the infection (Levy-Dweck, 2005).

Expanding Social Networks for Older Adults with HIV/AIDS

Older adults who have contracted HIV/AIDS may need different support systems to cope with the disease than younger populations due to the special social and psychological challenges facing older adults. The guilt and shame they experience may prevent them from disclosing the diagnosis to family and friends until the very end when death is imminent (Emlet, 2006b). For older gay men who have not disclosed their sexual orientation to family and friends or for older adults who have engaged in sex with prostitutes or had extramarital affairs, revealing the presence of HIV/ AIDS late in life may be seen as particularly risky. They may fear total rejection by family and friends at a time in their lives when social support is most crucial (Scrimshaw & Siegel, 2003). Being alienated from a spouse, partner, children, or grandchildren can be as psychologically devastating as the disease itself.

Support groups for families and friends of older adults with HIV/AIDS may be helpful in educating, encouraging, and empowering these groups to maintain important social connections with these older adults (Poindexter & Emlet, 2006). Older adults who have no support system or have lost support systems upon disclosing their HIV status may need a social worker's assistance in identifying and arranging support services in the community. Although older adults need time to grieve the loss of the support of family and friends, they most urgently need ongoing medical treatment, assistance with activities of daily living as the disease progresses, and financial and social support for treatment.

WHAT FACTORS PROMOTE HEALTHY AGING?

Although physical aging of the body is inevitable as persons grow older, disability and illness are not. The sole purpose of encouraging "healthy aging" is not to increase longevity. Rather, the goal of medicine and gerontology is to achieve the "compression of morbidity," defined as reducing the length and severity of illness and disability an older adult experiences in the last years of their lives. Since the early 1980s, gerontology and medicine have turned their research focus to learning about how people can maintain their health as they age. Two of the best-known studies have been the MacArthur Studies on Aging and the Harvard Study of Adult Development.

In 1984, the John D. and Catherine T. MacArthur Foundation brought together a group of scholars from assorted disciplines concerned with the aging process to design a long-term research project to study the positive aspects of the aging process and those older adults who were considered to be aging successfully. The combined effort of dozens of research projects conducted by physicians, biologists, geneticists, psychologists, sociologists, and others has come to be known as the MacArthur Study. It is the most comprehensive attempt to date to ascertain what constitutes successful aging and what individuals of all ages can do to promote good physical and psychological health in the later years (Rowe & Kahn, 1998).

Based on two important findings, the MacArthur Study has challenged both society's and medicine's assumptions that old age is a time of inevitable decline and disability (Rowe & Kahn, 1998). First, older adults are taking better care of themselves than ever before in history, through adjustments in diet and exercise. Second, the medical community is taking better care of older adults as it learns more about how to treat acute conditions, such as pneumonia and other infections, and how to help older adults minimize the debilitating effects of chronic conditions, such as arthritis, heart disease, and age-related losses in visual and auditory acuity. The study found that although a genetic predisposition to developing certain diseases, such as hypertension and heart disease, did affect an older adult's health, the influence of genetic predisposition becomes less important than lifestyle choices as an individual ages (Rowe & Kahn, 1998). In other words, genetic proclivity may put an older adult at risk for heart disease in his or her 60s, but diet, exercise, and other choices actually determine the course and disabling nature of the condition.

Dr. George E. Valliant, principal investigator of the Harvard Study of Adult Development, came to similar conclusions using data collected on the health and well-being of three cohorts of individuals between 1939 and 1999. Valliant and his colleagues found that many of the factors that predicted "healthy aging" in a person at age 80 were already established by age 50 (Valliant, 2002). The study found that ancestral longevity, one's cholesterol at age 50, nonfatal chronic diseases, early childhood experiences and temperament, and general social skills could not be used to predict an individual's longevity. Tobacco and alcohol use, normal weight, exercise, a happy life partnership, and a positive attitude about coping with life's challenges (what the study called mature defenses) were the best predictors of healthy aging. The good news is that most of these factors are controllable by individual choice.

The Influence of Diet

As people age, their metabolic rate slows down due to loss of lean muscle, meaning they burn fewer calories to perform the same activity. If older adults consume the same amount of food they did when they were younger without additional physical activity, weight gain is inevitable. Valliant (2002) found normal weight at age 50 to be strongly correlated with normal weight at age 80. Obesity, often the result of a combination of poor nutrition and inactivity, not only exacerbates existing health conditions but also promotes the development of cardiovascular problems that are genetically determined. The tendency to eat more than one's body needs may be the result of a lifetime of poor eating habits or the tendency to eat when one is bored rather than hungry.

The MacArthur Study found that older adults need a balanced diet low in fat and high in carbohydrates and protein to maintain good physical health (Rowe & Kahn, 1998). Although this finding is consistent with what nutritionists know about a healthy diet, older adults are at high risk for not eating enough of the right kinds of food to maintain health. Older adults may consume too many processed carbohydrates, such as those found in white bread, baked goods, or candy, and not enough of the complex carbohydrates found in peas, beans, and lentils. Complex carbohydrates can be helpful in promoting good bowel health and avoiding the tendency among older adults to experience constipation or other gastrointestinal problems. Older adults need more protein, as found in meats, fish, poultry, eggs, or dairy products, than younger people. Older adults are less likely to consume enough protein because it is one of the more expensive foods and because they may have difficulty chewing or swallowing meat. Vitamin and mineral supplements can be helpful in promoting good health among older adults who, unlike their younger counterparts, may not be getting sufficient vitamins in their daily diet. Antioxidants, discussed earlier in this chapter, are particularly important to an aging body to help cells fight the damaging effects of oxygen free radicals and to repair cellular damage caused by some diseases.

These findings suggest that older adults who make an active effort to eat a vitamin-rich diet high in protein and complex carbohydrates can prevent age-related physical changes from deteriorating into debilitating impairments. What is most encouraging is that even if older adults have had a poor diet throughout their lives and resign themselves to the belief that the damage is done, the human body begins to respond very quickly to changes in diet. Health and general well-being can be improved within a very short time with improved nutrition. Social workers can play an important role in working with nutritionists to provide nutrition education and counseling to older adults not only before but also after a serious health condition develops. These findings also suggest that congregate meal sites and mobile meals program need to pay more attention to developing lower-fat, higher-protein selections for older adults rather than those that contain too many processed carbohydrates, a less-expensive and more filling, but potentially damaging, dietary choice.

Exercise and Physical Activity

The MacArthur Study and the Harvard Study of Adult Development both confirmed the importance of physical activity and exercise for older adults, regardless of current health or mental health status. As the body ages, muscles weaken and become smaller, thereby affecting physical strength, sense of balance, and mobility. For most older adults, developing and maintaining physical fitness is not about taking up basketball at age 70. Rather, it is about maintaining the ability to walk comfortably and safely, to negotiate stairs, to reach up to shelves and cupboards, and to perform daily activities without becoming winded or injured. Unfortunately, as many older adults experience some loss of strength or endurance, they tend to engage in less physical activity and in that way promote a downward spiral in physical fitness. The phrase *use it or lose it* is a powerful adage!

Physical exercise is perhaps most helpful in its ability to cut the rate of coronary heart disease and diminish the risk of developing high blood pressure, two of the most dangerous physical problems older adults experience. Increased physical exercise protects against colon cancer, Type 2 diabetes, and osteoporosis when included as a component in a regimen of diet and medication. Even though some people believe that strenuous exercise causes arthritis, the MacArthur Study found that moderate regular exercise actually relieves arthritis pain and disability by promoting joint flexibility and general physical health. The MacArthur Study identified two forms of physical exercise that have shown dramatic results in slowing the physical deterioration of the aging body and promoting a general sense among older adults of feeling healthier and stronger.

Aerobic Exercise

Rapid walking, calisthenics, jogging, dancing, or working out on some exercise equipment is considered to be aerobic exercise, which is specifically aimed at increasing the heart rate for a certain amount of time to strengthen heart muscles. A stronger heart is more efficient and enjoys improved circulation and greater endurance. Older adults who regularly participate in aerobic exercise can be in better physical shape than sedentary middle-aged adults (Rowe & Kahn, 1998; Seeman & Chen, 2002). If designed with the special needs of the older adult in mind, aerobic exercise can be very safe for older adults, with little chance of serious injury or physical damage. Researchers found that even once-sedentary older adults can double their endurance within less than a year by participating in activities as simple as walking 45 minutes several times a week (Rowe & Kahn, 1998). The Harvard Study of Adult Development found that "some exercise," identified as simply as walking or swimming on a consistent basis throughout one's life, had a powerful effect on physical health as one grew older (Valliant, 2002). Older adults may not need to be regulars at a gym but rather incorporate some consistent physical activity into every day of their lives.

Strength Training

Weight training has become increasingly popular among all age groups and has shown great promise in helping older adults regain lost muscle strength. The MacArthur Study found that even the frailest of the oldest-old will respond to resistance training on weight machines or free weights. Strengthening muscles through weight training can help an older adult lose weight by increasing his or her metabolic rate. Strength training for older adults has proven to increase muscle mass, therefore increasing not only general muscle strength but also improving balance, gait, and an older adult's general health (Seguin, Epping, Buchner, Block, & Nelson, 2002). One of the side effects not anticipated by researchers in the MacArthur Study was the positive influence of weight training on an older adult's mental health. Those involved in weight training were less likely to become or remain depressed than older adults who were not involved in this kind of exercise.

The importance of physical exercise and physical activity in minimizing the debilitating effects of physical aging are very encouraging to both social workers and others who develop intervention efforts for older adults. Any intervention should include opportunities for older adults to begin (or continue) some form of physical activity that appeals to them. This is one of those situations where social workers can play an important role in taking on the role of coach! Connecting older adults to physical activities that give them the opportunity to push their own physical abilities as well as to have fun doing it with other older adults promises both physical and psychological benefits.

Fall Prevention

The risk of falling and sustaining an injury increases dramatically with age due to general physical fragility, impaired vision, muscle weakness, or even occasional confusion among some older adults (American Geriatrics Society, 2011). Even older adults who are healthy and active can be at risk. A serious head injury or broken hip can be a life-changing event, resulting in hospitalization or premature nursing home placement. The effort to prevent falls is considered one of the factors in promoting healthy aging. The American Geriatrics Society (AGS) (2011) revised its clinical practice guidelines for preventing falls to include a falls risk assessment for all older adults even those who do not report unsteady gait or an actually fall within the last 12 months. These recommendations include a visual inspection of an older adult's feet and footwear, the clinician's and older adult's assessment of functional ability and a frank discussion of real and perceived threats to the safety of the older adult's home environment. The AGS recommends a complete review of medications to identify possible side effects that may include weakness or light-headedness and reduce the levels of medication, if possible. The organization also recommends customizing an exercise program for each older adult aimed at strengthening muscles in the back, legs, and feet, those responsible for posture and gait, and encourage older adults to wear proper footwear. Treating vision impairments such as cataracts as well as managing low blood pressure and cardiac abnormalities which can cause weakness or cause brief moments of unconsciousness are other factors shown to reduce the incidence of falls in older adults. The AGS also recommends that all older adults have their home environments assessed for fall hazards, a topic that will be covered in Chapter 4.

Psychosocial Factors

The importance of good nutrition and physical exercise are self-evident as important factors in promoting healthy aging. Researchers have also found that a number of psychosocial factors have a direct influence on promoting healthy aging or, when an older adult already has a chronic health condition, minimizing its effect on an older adult's quality of life. Older adults with even low levels of depression are more likely to be plagued by physical illness and show shorter life expectancies (Cooper, Harris, & McGready, 2002). It is reasonable to raise the question of whether an illness has caused the depression or whether the depression has enhanced the physical illness. Regardless, there is a clear connection between physical illness and depression, suggesting that treating (or preventing) depression can improve physical health in older adults. Interventions for reducing depression are covered in detail in Chapter 6.

Being married or in a supportive partnership is correlated not only with a longer life expectancy but with better physical and mental health (Cooper, Harris, & McGready, 2002) although this is significant for men but not for women. The presence of social and emotional support, perhaps better health habits, and caring for or being cared by another person are identified as the direct benefits of being part of a couple in older adulthood. It is important to recognize that women are more likely to be caregivers rather than care receivers, which may explain the difference between men and women in the health benefits of being married or partnered. As will be explored in Chapter 12, caregiving can pose a serious threat to one's health and well-being.

Resilience, the ability to adapt to and thrive despite life's adversities, has also been identified as a predictive factor in healthy aging (Harris, 2008). Those older adults who have functioned relatively well despite financial hardship, chaotic social and familial environments, and personal losses appear to do better with the health changes that accompany older adulthood. There is some truth to the observations that some older adults are "tough old birds." While resilience is usually associated with childhood experiences, it continues to be a factor in an individual's adjustment to the challenges of any life stage. Included in the discussion of resilience is the equally important personal characteristic of self-efficacy or the self-perception that one continues to have the ability to be effective in determining certain factors in one's life (Seeman & Chen, 2002). Older adults who see a health problem as something they play a part in managing, rather than simply succumbing to, are more likely to have better health outcomes and be less disabled by the condition. This is a further indication of using the strengths perspective in working with older adults. Social workers can help empower older adults to be proactive, rather than reactive, in managing their own health.

SUMMARY

The job of a gerontological social worker is to view every older adult within a complex biopsychosocial context. This chapter has addressed the biological changes associated with the aging process, some of which are universal to all aging persons and others that are considered pathological. All of the vital physiological systems are affected by the aging process as the body becomes less efficient in replacing worn and damaged cells. Age-related changes in vision, the neurological system, the gastrointestinal system, and the urinary tract depend on general health and genetic endowment, whereas cardiovascular, dermatological, respiratory, and hearing changes may be hastened by the accumulative effects of lifelong personal habits.

Urinary incontinence is not a normal part of the aging process, but older adults experience the problem more frequently than do their younger counterparts. Left untreated, incontinence may lead to social isolation, medical complications, and loss of independence, all issues of vital concern to a gerontological social worker. As the majority of cases of incontinence can be effectively treated, it is important for social work professionals to recognize the significance of incontinence as a problem for some older adults and to encourage them to seek aggressive treatment for the condition.

The growing incidence of new cases of HIV/AIDS among the aging population suggests social work will play an increasingly important role in promoting preventative education to older adults. Dispelling prejudicial myths about the infection through preventative education, encouraging early diagnosis and treatment, and developing age-specific community support systems for HIV-positive older adults are compassionate and effective ways to respond to the HIV/AIDS crisis in the older adult population.

The most encouraging news about the biological process of aging and ways in which to minimize the debilitating effects of physical changes come from the MacArthur Study and the Harvard Study of Adult Development, research efforts aimed at identifying those factors that contribute to healthy aging. Through a program of diet and exercise, older adults can prevent as well as reverse physical impairment caused by age-related conditions. Social work plays a significant role in incorporating nutrition counseling, fall prevention, physical activity, and good mental health as part of any intervention plan for older adults.

References

Administration on Aging. (1999). *National Institute on Aging age page: Taking care of your teeth and mouth.* Washington, DC: Author. Retrieved August 2, 1999, from http://www.nia.nih.gov/health/publication/taking-care-your-teeth-and-mouth

Administration on Aging. (2003). *A view close-up: AIDS & older Americans.* Washington, DC: Author. Retrieved April 1, 2003, from http://www.aoa.gov/AoARoot/AoA_Programs/HPW/HIV_AIDS/index.aspx

Aldwin, C. M., & Gilmer, D. F. (2004). *Health, illness, and optimal aging: Biological and psychosocial perspectives.* Thousand Oaks, CA: Sage.

American Geriatrics Society. (2011). Summary of the updated American Geriatrics Society/British Geriatrics Society clinical practice guideline for prevention of falls in older persons. *Journal of the American Geriatrics Society, 59,* 148–157.

American Heart Association. (2011). *Cardiovascular disease statistics.* Retrieved May 17, 2011, from http://www.americanheart.org

Arthritis Foundation. (2007). *Osteoarthritis: What is it?* Retrieved August 3, 2007, from http://www.arthritis.org

Assad, L. A. D. (2000). Urinary incontinence in older men. *Topics in Geriatric Rehabilitation, 16*(1), 33–53.

Aupperle, P. (1996). Medical issues. In K. M. Nokes (Ed.), *HIV/AIDS and the older adult* (pp. 25–32). Washington, DC: Taylor & Francis.

Bachus, M. A. (1998). HIV and the older adult. *Journal of Gerontological Nursing, 24*(11), 41–46.

Baum, T., Capezuti, E., & Driscoll, G. (2002). Falls. In V. T. Cotter & N. E. Strumpf (Eds.), *Advanced practice nursing with older adults: Clinical guidelines* (pp. 245–270). New York: McGraw-Hill.

Brandeis, G. H., Bauman, M. M., Hossain, M., Morris, J. N., & Resnick, N. M. (1997). The prevalence of potentially remediable urinary incontinence in frail older people: A study using the Minimum Data Set. *Journal of the American Geriatric Society, 45*, 179–184.

Brown, D. R. (1997). *Cultural mistrust among African Americans: Results from the AIDS Awareness and Behavior Survey*. Detroit, MI: Wayne State University, Center for Urban Studies.

Brown, D. R., & Sankar, A. (1998). HIV/AIDS and aging minority populations. *Research on Aging, 20*(6), 865–885.

Centers for Disease Control and Prevention. (2003). *HIV/AIDS populations-at-risk: The elderly*. Rockville, MD: Centers for Disease Control, National Prevention Information Network. Retrieved November 18, 2003, from http://www.cdcnpin.org/scripts/population/elderly.asp

Centers for Disease Control and Prevention. (2005a). *Bone health: Osteoporosis*. Rockville, MD: Centers for Disease Control and Prevention. Retrieved January 22, 2008, from http: www.cdc.gov/nccdphp/dnpa/nutrition_for_everyone/bonehealth

Centers for Disease Control Prevention. (2005b). *HIV/AIDS surveillance report 2004* (Vol. 16). Atlanta, GA: Author

Centers for Disease Control and Prevention, The Merck Company Foundation. (2007). *The state of aging and health in America 2007*. Whitehouse Station, NJ: The Merck Company Foundation.

Cooper, J. K., Harris, Y., & McGready, J. (2002). Sadness predicts death in older people. *Journal of Aging and Health, 14*(4), 509–526.

Crisologo, S., Campbell, M. H., & Forte, J. A. (1996). Social work, AIDS, and the elderly: Current knowledge and practice. *Journal of Gerontological Social Work, 26*(1/2), 49–70.

Effros, R. B. (2001). Immune system activity. In E. J. Masoro & S. N. Austad (Eds.), *Handbook of the biology of aging* (pp. 324–353). San Diego, CA: Academic Press.

Eliopoulos, C. (2005). *Gerontological nursing* (6th ed.). Philadelphia: Lippincott, Williams & Wilkins.

Emlet, C. A. (2006a). You're awfully old to have this disease: Experiences of stigma and ageism in adults 50 years and older living with HIV/AIDS. *The Gerontologist, 46*(6), 781–790.

Emlet, C. A. (2006b). A comparison of HIV-stigma and disclosure patterns between older and younger adults living with HIV/AIDS. *AIDS Patient Care and STDs, 20*, 350–358.

Emlet, C. A., & Farkas, K. J. (2002). Correlates of service utilization among midlife and older adults with HIV/AIDS: The role of age in the equation. *Journal of Aging and Health, 14*, 315–335.

Finch, C. E. (1991). *Longevity: Senescence and the genome*. Chicago: University of Chicago Press.

Grune, R., & Davies, K. J. A. (2001). Oxidative process in aging. In E. J. Masoro & S. N. Austad (Eds.), *Handbook of the biology of aging* (pp. 25–58). San Diego, CA: Academic Press.

Gulya, A. J. (1995). Ear disorders. In W. B. Abrams, M. H. Beers, & R. Berkow (Eds.), *The Merck manual of geriatrics* (2nd ed., pp. 1315–1342). Whitehouse Station, NJ: Merck Research Laboratories.

Harris, P. B. (2008). Another wrinkle in the debate about successful aging: The undervalued concept of resilience and the lived experience of dementia. *International Journal of Aging and Human Development, 67*(1), 43–61.

Harvard Gazette Archives. (2001). Scientists identify chromosome location of genes associated with long life. *Harvard University Gazette*. Retrieved August 5, 2007, from http://www.news.harvard.edu/gazette/2001/08.16/chromosomes.html

Hayflick, L. (1994). *How and why we age*. New York: Ballantine.

Hill-O'Neill, K. A., & Shaughnessy, M. (2002). Dizziness and stroke. In V. T. Cotter & N. E. Strumpf (Eds.), *Advanced practice nursing with older adults: Clinical guidelines* (pp. 163–181). New York: McGraw-Hill.

Hooyman, N., & Kiyak, H. A. (2002). *Social gerontology* (6th ed.). Boston: Allyn & Bacon.

Legato, M. L. (1997). *Gender specific aspects of human biology for the practicing physician*. Armonk, NY: Futura.

Levy-Dweck, S. (2005). HIV/AIDS fifty and older: A hidden and growing population. *Journal of Gerontological Social Work, 46*(2), 37–49.

McCormick, A. M., & Campisi, J. (1991). Cellular aging and senescence. *Current Opinion in Cell Biology, 3*, 230–234.

Melville, J. L., Katon, W., Delaney, K., & Newton, K. (2005). Urinary incontinence in U.S. women: A population-based study. *Archives of Internal Medicine, 165*(5), 537–542.

Militades, H., & Kaye, L. W. (2006). Older adults with orthopedic and mobility restrictions. In B. Berkman (Ed.), *Handbook of social work in health and aging* (pp. 41–51). New York: Oxford.

National Association on HIV over Fifty. (2007). *HIV/AIDS and older adults*. Boston: Author. Retrieved August 3, 2007, from http://www.hivoverfifty.org

National Center for Biotechnology Information. (2010). *Osteoporosis*. Retrieved April 19, 2011, from http://www.ncbi.nlm.nih.gov/pubmedhealth/PMH0001400/

National Institute on Aging. (2000). *Foot care*. Washington, DC: Author. Retrieved August 3, 2007, from http://www.nia.nih.gov/health/publication/foot-care

National Institute on Aging. (2007). *HIV/AIDS and older people* [Age page]. Washington, DC: Author. Retrieved August 8, 2007, from http://www.nia.nih.gov/health/publication/hiv-aids-and-older-people

Newman, D. K., & Palmer, M. H. (2003). State of the science on urinary incontinence. *American Journal of Nursing, 3*, 1–58.

Nokes, K. M. (1996). Health care needs. In K. M. Nokes (Ed.), *HIV/AIDS and the older adult* (pp. 1–8). Washington, DC: Taylor & Francis.

Ouslander, J. G. (1983). Incontinence and nursing homes: Epidemiology and management. *The Gerontologist, 23*, 257.

Palmer, M. H. (1996). *Urinary continence: Assessment and promotion*. Gaithersburg, MD: Aspen.

Poindexter, C., & Emlet, C. (2006). HIV-infected and HIV-affected older adults. In B. Berkman (Ed.), *The handbook of social work in health and aging* (pp. 91–102). New York: Oxford University Press.

Rose, M. A. (1996). Effect of an AIDS education program for older adults. *Journal of Community Health Nursing, 13*(3), 141–148.

Rowe, J. W., & Kahn, R. L. (1998). *Successful aging*. New York: Pantheon.

Scrimshaw, E. W., & Siegel, K. (2003). Perceived barriers to social support from family and friends among older adults with HIV/AIDS. *Journal of Health Psychology, 8*, 738–752.

Seeman, T., & Chen, X. (2002). Risk and protective factors for physical functioning in older adults with and without chronic conditions: MacArthur studies of successful aging. *Journal of Gerontology: Social Sciences, 57B*(3), S135–S144.

Seguin, R. A., Epping, J. N., Buchner, D., Block, R., & Nelson, M. E. (2002). *Growing stronger: Strength training for older adults*. Washington, DC: Centers for Disease Control and Prevention and Tufts University.

Specht, J. K. P. (2005). Nine myths of incontinence in older adults. *American Journal of Nursing, 105*(6), 58–68.

Spirduso, W. W. (1995). *Physical dimensions of aging*. Champaign, IL: Human Kinetics.

Strassburg, S., Springer, J., & Anker, S. S. (2005). Muscle wasting in cardiac cachexia. *International Journal of Biochemistry and Cell Biology, 37*, 1938–1947.

Strombeck, R., & Levy, J. A. (1998). Educational strategies and interventions targeting adults age 50 and older for HIV/AIDS prevention. *Research on Aging, 20*(6), 912–937.

Stuen, C. (2006). Older adults with age-related sensory loss. In B. Berkman (Ed.) *Handbook on social work in health and aging* (pp. 65–77). New York: Oxford University Press.

Styrcula, L. (2001). Under cover no more: Plain talk about mature sexuality. *Nursing Spectrum, 11*(12DC), 16–17.

Swenson, N. M., & Siegal, D. L. (1994). Urinary incontinence. In P. B. Doress-Worters & D. L. Siegal (Eds.), *The new growing older: Women aging with knowledge and power* (pp. 300–314). New York: Simon and Schuster.

Tabloski, P. A. (2010). *Gerontological nursing* (2nd ed.). Upper Saddle River, NJ: Prentice Hall.

Timaris, P. S. (1988). *Psychologic bases of geriatrics*. New York: Macmillan.

Tockman, M. S. (1995). The effects of aging on the lungs: Lung cancer. In W. B. Abrams, M. H. Beers, & R. Berkow (Eds.), *The Merck manual of geriatrics* (2nd ed., pp. 569–574). Whitehouse Station, NJ: Merck Research Laboratories.

Umlauf, M. G., & Sherman, S. M. (1996). Symptoms of urinary incontinence among older community-dwelling men. *Journal of Wound, Ostomy and Continence Nurses Society, 23*(6), 314–321.

United States National Library of Medicine and National Institutes of Health. (2011). *Antioxidants.* Retrieved April 19, 2011, from http://www.nlm.nih.gov/medlineplus/antioxidants.html

Valliant, G. E. (2002). *Aging well: The Harvard study of adult development.* New York: Little, Brown and Company.

Young, J. B. (2001). Effects of aging on the sympathoadrenal system. In E. J. Masoro & S. N. Austad (Eds.), *Handbook of the biology of aging* (pp. 269–296). San Diego, CA: Academic Press.

The following questions will test your application and analysis
of the content found within this chapter.

1. The guidelines for fall prevention outlined by the American Geriatric Society
   a. state that falls are inevitable for all older adults.
   b. cite physicians as responsible for preventing falls.
   c. suggest that fall prevention is a combination of preventative medicine and developing an older adult's physical strength.
   d. advocate for new medicines to be developed to prevent falls.

2. An older adult may take longer to answer a direct question due to
   a. neurological changes.
   b. cardiovascular changes.
   c. hearing and vision changes.
   d. metabolic system changes.

3. An older adult refuses to use a cane or walker even though he is very unsteady on his feet and has a history of frequent falls. He lives alone but goes out daily to a congregate meal site. What should the social worker do?

4. An older woman has been diagnosed with arthritis in her knees and feels she needs to stay home in order not to "wear her knees out" despite her doctor's recommendation she take at least a short walk every day. She is becoming increasingly isolated. What should the social worker do?

Psychosocial Adjustments to Aging

Competencies Applied with Practice Behaviors Examples —In This Chapter

☑ Professional Identity

❑ Ethical Practice

☑ Critical Thinking

☑ Diversity in Practice

❑ Human Rights & Justice

❑ Research-Based Practice

☑ Human Behavior

❑ Policy Practice

❑ Practice Contexts

❑ Engage, Assess, Intervene, Evaluate

The biological changes accompanying the aging process described in Chapter 2 are the most visible signs that the body is growing older. The degree to which these physical changes cause functional impairment is due to a combination of genetic luck, exposure to disease and illness, and lifestyle choices. This chapter explores the psychosocial changes that accompany the biological changes—those adjustments in cognitive functioning, intellectual ability, and social behavior that determine how people think and act as they grow older. Psychological and social patterns of adjustment are incredibly diverse from older adult to older adult. Some older adults never experience a noticeable loss of memory or lessening of ability to perform complex tasks, even well into their 90s and beyond. They are able to maintain active, energetic lives deeply connected to family and friends. Other older adults begin to experience serious memory loss as early as 60 years of age or withdraw from social interaction to wait to die. The path of psychosocial changes is profoundly affected by a combination of inherent personality traits, physical health, and the quality of the relationships an older adult has with others in his or her environment.

This chapter begins with a look at the psychological changes, including changes in cognitive and intellectual abilities, that are most commonly seen in older adults. Older adults' sexuality is presented as a crucial aspect of psychosocial functioning, despite the erroneous assumptions by families and helping professionals that older adults are no longer interested in sexual activity. This section is followed by an examination of a variety of social theories of aging that speculate about what behavior patterns are commonly observed in older adults as they adapt to new and unfamiliar social roles and relationships. Once these adjustments have been identified, it is important to consider what implications those changes have for gerontological social work. The chapter concludes with a look at the findings about psychosocial changes in aging observed in the MacArthur Study and the Harvard Study of Adult Development, the most recent and comprehensive attempts to determine what constitutes successful or optimal aging.

PSYCHOLOGICAL CHANGES THAT ACCOMPANY AGING

Although the biological changes that accompany the aging process are often the most noticeable (and sometimes most bothersome), changes that occur in cognitive and emotional functioning are often those most feared by older adults. At the first sign of forgetfulness, middle-aged and older adults may question if they are losing their minds or showing the first signs of Alzheimer's disease. Families worry about an aging relative's ability to follow a complicated regimen of multiple prescriptions. Some older adults learn computer skills very quickly and are active in using the Internet and e-mail to stay connected to the world. This section of the chapter discusses normal age-related changes in cognitive functioning and personality. The psychological and emotional disorders associated with aging are discussed in Chapter 5.

Cognitive changes are those that occur in the intellectual, memory, learning, and creative processes of older adults. Do people actually get smarter as they grow older and accumulate knowledge and experience? Is it inevitable that older adults will experience memory problems, forgetting what they had for lunch but remembering details about events from their childhood? Can older adults learn new skills? These are complex questions about very complicated cognitive functions, the answers of which are both "yes" and "no."

Intelligence

Intelligence is the way in which a person gathers information, processes it, develops new ideas, and applies information to new and familiar situations in the activities of daily living. There are two major aspects of intelligence. It follows that as people grow older and accumulate knowledge and experience that they should know more. Planning a garden, reading, cooking, and repair work are all examples of activities that require knowledge acquired from a lifetime of experiences. From the perspective of accumulating information, intelligence does increase or at least is maintained well into old age. Psychologists refer to this type of intelligence as *crystallized intelligence* (Salthouse, 2000). How effectively individuals accumulate knowledge is strongly influenced by the amount of information they are exposed to through education and life experience and, to some degree, genetic luck (Hawley, Cherry, Su, Chiu, & Jazwinski, 2006). In terms of accumulated knowledge, older adults do become smarter. They do know more than when they were younger. Intelligence testing that measures the recall of accumulated knowledge tests crystallized intelligence.

However, determining how to live on a single fixed income or negotiate public transportation after a lifetime of driving—challenges that accompany life changes, such as retirement and widowhood—requires a different set of intellectual skills. The ability to secure new information, combine it with accumulated knowledge, and apply it to problem solving is known as fluid intelligence (Salthouse, 2000; Schaie, 1996). Older adults do not perform as well on intelligence testing measures that measure problem-solving competence or the ability to perform a sequence of tasks. There is no clear evidence that age alone accounts for poor performance in this area of intelligence testing. Most intelligence testing is timed, and older adults have a slower reaction time due to deterioration in the neurotransmitters, which was discussed in the previous chapter on biological aspects of aging. When time restrictions are lifted from intelligence testing situations, there are only negligible differences between younger and older subjects (Hawley et al., 2006; Salthouse, 2000).

Factors Contributing to Intelligence

Intellectual functioning in old age is the product of a variety of factors, a few of which are not related to the aging process at all. Genetic ability may be the most important determinant of all (Waldstein, 2000). Individuals who show high intellectual functioning throughout their lives are most likely to continue to function well in their later years. Higher levels of education and the choice of challenging life work contribute to maintaining or enhancing intellectual abilities as a person ages (Snowdon, 2001). In general, innate abilities combined with a lifetime of intellectual exercise are strong predictors of how well intellectual functioning will stand the test of time.

The primary mental abilities associated with intelligence are verbal understanding, spatial relationships, reasoning, and basic fluency in both words and numbers. These activities are those most important to daily functioning for people of all ages. Competence in these areas continues to improve until the late 30s and early 40s. In the absence of disease, primary mental abilities remain stable until the late 60s, when a slow, and in some cases almost indiscernible, process of decline begins (Waldstein, 2000). By the late 70s, this decline is more noticeable in some older adults, but still negligible in others.

Age-related changes in physical health, sensory acuity, and nutrition and the presence of depression have also been associated with a decline in intellectual functioning. Cardiovascular disease, characterized by impaired blood circulation, has been linked to observable changes in an older adult's ability to engage in complex problem-solving activities (Waldstein & Elias, 2000). Although the efficiency of nerves in carrying messages from the brain is compromised as the body ages, blood circulation also plays a role in general overall healthy functioning of the brain. Sensory input from vision and hearing are an important part of processing information. When these functions are impaired in older adults, cognitive functioning is also compromised. Older adults may appear not to follow a conversation or a task because they are missing important environmental stimuli. What is especially difficult is that older adults may not know they are missing this input and adamantly deny that they are having trouble.

Nutrition

Inadequate nutrition contributes to declining intellectual functioning (Leventhal, Rabin, Leventhal, & Burns, 2001). Biological changes in the esophagus and stomach result in older adults feeling "full" sooner than younger persons, which may result in either insufficient caloric intake or vitamin deficiency. The brain simply does not function as efficiently without adequate nutrients. The social interaction derived from eating with others has been found to improve not only appetite but also mood, intellectual functioning, and subjective well-being. "Meals nourish our heart, mind, and soul as well as our bodies" (Snowdon, 2001, p. 170). Along with insufficient nutrition, older adults are more prone to dehydration because of a diminished sense of thirst or a tendency to restrict fluid intake to avoid frequent urination. The severe dangers of inadequate nutrition and dehydration will be covered in greater detail in Chapter 5, when the organic brain condition, delirium, is discussed.

The Environment

One of the most important findings about intellectual functioning among older adults is the significance of the environment in which older adults are required to use cognitive skills. Older adults who show poor intellectual functioning in the testing environment of a laboratory are likely to function better in more familiar environments, such as their own homes. Ultimately, the ability to engage in problem solving in the challenges of everyday life is infinitely more important in understanding an older adult's cognitive functioning. Research indicates that when elders engage in problem solving that has immediate relevance to their daily functioning, they remain amazingly adept at rallying cognitive resources (Wahl, 2001; Willis, 1996). These same studies have found that retaining one's independence is the strongest motivator for older adults to find creative ways to solve problems. If maintaining their independence is contingent on the ability to follow a complicated prescription regimen, older adults may compensate by writing detailed notes about what medication is to be taken at what time of the day. Posting notes around the kitchen helps to remind them to make sure the gas is turned off or the doors are locked. This type of behavior is familiar to those who have worked with older adults and represents an older adult's own efforts to compensate for cognitive losses. The importance of a familiar environment also helps to explain why older adults may lose cognitive functioning rapidly in unfamiliar environments, such as specialized housing or a nursing home.

Personality

Personality is an individual's composite of innate and learned behaviors and emotional and cognitive functions that determines how that individual interacts with the environment. This includes emotions, moods, coping strategies, and a sense of subjective well-being. From the moment of birth, individuals begin to show their own unique personalities. Some individuals are by nature easygoing, upbeat, and pleasant, whereas others are intense, have guarded emotionality, and may be less sociable. Although people cannot choose their personality styles, they can control their own behavior. In a sense, personality is both structure and process. It is structure in that an individual's personality remains relatively stable throughout life, and it is a process in that it is always changing in response to the environment. In childhood, adolescence, and young adulthood, the personality is relatively flexible and is in constant interaction with the environment in the process of maturation. During adulthood, the mature personality becomes more stable and, in the absence of disease, is less likely to change radically (Ryff, Kwan, & Singer, 2001).

Psychosocial Tasks

Erik Erikson believed that the personality adapts throughout life in response to a set of psychosocial tasks, or challenges, that accompany the individual's development in the environment (Erikson, 1963). From the first challenge a child faces in developing trust or distrust in those around him or her, Erikson saw the interaction between the genetic endowment of the personality and the context of the environment. He believed that if people are to move through each of the life stages successfully it is necessary to resolve the psychosocial crises germane to that stage. He hypothesized that if early life crises were not resolved, problems in psychosocial functioning would appear later in people's lives. For example, if people have not learned to trust as infants, it is difficult for them to develop intimacy with another person later in life. The final life stage in Erikson's work—seen as the work of old age—is resolving the crisis between ego integrity and ego despair. In this stage, individuals must learn to accept all that has happened in their lives and to come to an understanding about what meaning their lives have had. Sometimes that process involves taking care of unfinished business and changing what can be changed, such as repairing damaged relationships. Other times that means letting go of those things that cannot be changed.

Menniger (1999) expanded the discussion of the psychosocial tasks of old age to more specific challenges. These include accepting the revised sense of one's physical self as a result of the physical changes associated with aging, accepting the loss of peers and significant others, facing the potential loss of independence, and resolving the dissonance between the preretirement image of oneself with the postretirement self. Successfully accomplishing these tasks is part of the process of developing ego integrity. Achieving what is often referred to as environmental mastery is a lifelong process and an essential part of understanding the dynamic nature of the human personality.

In the most recent work on adult development, Valliant (2002) modifies Erikson's original eight stages, expanding specifically on the adult life tasks. He begins with the adult life task of achieving identity, a sense of oneself and one's values as preparation for separating from one's family of origin. Achieving individual identity is required for the next stage of intimacy, expanding the sense of self to include an "other," which can include either an intimate partner or other close adult friendships. He describes the next life task as career consolidation, an identity associated with one's social role in the world of work or productive and meaningful activity. These life tasks are similar to those identified by Erikson but Valliant adds another task to adult development, that of mastering generativity, the capacity to guide the next generation through giving of oneself (Valliant, 2002). By *generativity*, Valliant means community building, with the adult serving as a consultant, coach, or mentor to younger adults. In his study, older adults who were able to develop opportunities to enhance their connection to their community and younger adults were three times as likely to find satisfaction and joy in their later years. Connected to generativity is the life task of becoming *a keeper of meaning*. Valliant describes this life task as the development of an older adult's passion for preserving or enhancing something that is dear to him or her, such as a religious tradition, social cause, or legacy of accomplishment. Pursuing something that is meaningful and works to preserve something important can be an active way for people to avoid social isolation and continue to contribute to society. The adult's final adult life task is that of achieving integrity, which he defines similarly to Erikson, the acceptance of one's life as it was and was meant to be. Valliant suggests these modifications to Erikson's original psychosocial life tasks in an effort to not only understand the complexity of the psychological work older adults face but also identify that there is tremendous opportunity for older adults to continue growing and changing. The later years of an individual's life can clearly be ones of satisfaction and joy when these tasks can be mastered.

Coping with Stress

Meeting the psychosocial tasks of old age creates stress for older adults. How an individual handles stress is affected by both inherent personality traits and behaviors learned in facing stressful events throughout one's life (Ryff, Kwan, & Singer 2001; Valliant, 2002).

Ryff et al. (2001) identified a six-factor model of psychological well-being that contributes to an older adult's ability to cope with stress and manage the psychosocial tasks of older adulthood. Three of these factors, self-acceptance, the ability to identify one's purpose in life, and opportunities for personal growth, are clearly rooted in an individual's personality structure. The other three factors, positive relationships with others, a sense of environmental mastery, and a sense of autonomy (the ability to follow one's own convictions as opposed to being a follower), are contingent on the older adult's relationship with the social environment. These six personality factors are powerful predictors of the likelihood that an older adult will react to stressful events with either optimism or depression (Monopoli, Vaccaro, Christmann, & Badgett, 2000).

Lazarus and Cohen (1977) found that the quality of an older adult's response to stress was contingent on four elements. The first is "cognitive appraisal" of a situation—that is, whether older adults perceive a situation to be stressful at all. For some older adults, a late morning paper will ruin their entire day, whereas for other older adults, it would take a life-threatening event to arouse much anxiety. Some older adults are very good at "not sweating the small stuff"; others look for the small stuff to worry about. A second component is how desirable or undesirable the stressful event appears to an older adult. One older adult might approach a knee replacement as a welcome end to chronic knee pain and accept an uncomfortable recovery as just part of the process that ultimately will have positive consequences. Another older adult might have a hard time seeing beyond the painful recovery period to the benefits of a more comfortable joint. People's personalities give them a different set of lens through which to observe similar events, and thus they have different reactions. A third component in how older adults adapt to stress is the availability of a support system. Those older adults with partners or extensive family and friend support networks appear to handle stress better because they do not feel they are alone. Being able to rally emotional support from others seems to mitigate the effects of stress. A fourth component is the amount of control people feel they have in responding to stress.

Ruth and Coleman (1996) found that older adults face greater stress in association with everyday existence. Maintaining a household, coping with limitations imposed by physical illness, and eating alone are examples of events that are likely to cause ongoing stress that is as difficult as, if not more than, major life transitions.

Memory

In the absence of disease, the human brain has almost unlimited capacity for memory. That capacity is not affected by age-related changes in memory. Rather, it is the process by which the human mind remembers that changes as the body ages (Craik, 2000). There are three components to memory. Sensory memory is what people notice and commit to memory through the senses. A favorite song, the smell of fresh baked bread, and the sight of a beautiful sunset are examples of sensory memory. One does not decide to remember those things but simply does so because the image has made an impression on sensory memory. Sensory memory is the first step in processing information and involves receiving information through one of the five senses. Words and images are first seen through vision. Sounds are heard and often connected to visual images. The smell of fresh bread, for example, stimulates the memory without vision or sound. Touch, the last of the five senses, plays a role in helping older adults notice texture or temperature. Sensory memory itself is not affected by age-related changes, although the ability to recognize these sensory images may be impaired when any of the senses are impaired by age-related changes. Older adults may not recognize a song because they cannot hear it clearly or may not recognize the smell of fresh bread because they cannot smell it. Smells are a very powerful stimulus for memory and will be discussed later in this book in the section describing the use of reminiscence therapy with older adults. Perceiving information from the environment through the senses is a precursor to committing information to memory (Craik, 2000; Craik & Jennings, 1992).

Another component of memory is called primary memory, or what is known as a person's working memory. Primary memory requires that an individual encode a memory and commit it to storage (Craik, 2000). For example, much of the information you are exposed to as a student starts in primary memory. To be able to access that information later, you must be aware of it, be motivated to remember it, and store it along with similar information. This is not entirely a conscious process. The greater the incentive to remember the information and the more deliberate the effort to remember it, however, the more likely that information will be committed to the third component of memory, secondary memory. Secondary memory is the accumulation of information that is stored until it is retrieved through recall. If the information is reinforced, it becomes part of a person's long-term memory.

For many older adults, it is not the capacity to remember that is impaired with aging, but, rather, the processing of resources that result in remembering. Perceptual speed decreases, making it harder to process information in the same length of time as when the individual was younger (Smith, 1996). For example, when a physician very quickly reviews a number of prescriptions, it may be difficult for an older patient to process both the visual and auditory clues and connect them to a specific medication. Is it the blue pill that is taken twice a day but only with food, or is it the white pill? For many older adults, too much information given too quickly cannot be processed efficiently enough to be worked through the working memory and committed to secondary memory. This information overload results in older adults' inability to remember—not because of reduced memory capacity but because of a difficulty in processing this information into memory.

The Motivation to Remember

The motivation to remember information also plays an important role in the process of memory for older adults (Willis, 1996). Why do older adults forget what they had for lunch but remember infinite details about holidays with their families 50 years ago? What one had for lunch lasts in sensory memory only for a limited time. Unless there is some significance to remembering it, it probably will not be remembered (even by much younger persons). However, the memory of holiday celebrations with family members is important. These memories may have been recalled and rehearsed frequently throughout life. This reinforces that memory. When memories are reinforced by strong emotions, they are deeply embedded in secondary memory. The combination of sensory memories and strong emotional memories makes this type of memory more significant and therefore more easily remembered. Unfortunately, older adults may resign themselves to more memory loss than actually affects them, having internalized the notion that memory always deteriorates with age (Rozencwajg et al., 2005). If an older adult expects his or her memory to fail, it probably will.

Recognition of objects and names is easier for older adults than strict recall of factual material. Giving people environmental clues to help them remember things such as a clock or a calendar facilitates memory. When asked to recall infrequently used information, older adults may take longer than a younger person to access that information from

Figure 3.1 • What Do You Remember?

Answer the following questions without consulting any other resource other than your memory. At some time you have known the answers to all these questions. How much do you remember?

1. What is the capitol of the state of South Dakota?
2. Who won the Super Bowl last year?
3. Who was your first grade teacher? Your fourth grade teacher?
4. What was your phone number when you were growing up?
5. Why is the sky blue?

Why did you remember the answer to some of these questions and not others? What answers would you remember if you had more time to think? What answers may never have made it into your long-term memory? What role does motivation play in remembering the answers to these questions?

secondary memory (Figure 3.1). It is not that they cannot access the memory but that it simply takes longer. This "tip of the tongue" phenomenon occurs for most people long before they become older and is the result of the decreasing efficiency of the process of memory recall (Willis, 1996).

Learning

Adults learn in ways different from the ways children do. Young children are often described as "sponges" soaking up knowledge almost effortlessly, without necessarily questioning why they have to learn it. Adults, on the other hand, learn better when the information or skill they have to learn has some very specific relevance for their lives. Their motivation to learn is based on meeting a specific need for that knowledge rather than simply for the exercise of committing knowledge to memory (Vella, 2000). Adults also learn more effectively when they have an opportunity to rehearse new behavior or information. The process of reinforcement is an essential part of adult learning. These two factors—relevance to one's life and the opportunity to rehearse new behavior—are significant factors in an older adult's ability to learn. It is not surprising that older adults perform poorly on laboratory experiments in learning when asked to memorize long lists of words or numbers (Willis, 1996). Older adults appear to be more discriminating learners and need to see the relevance of the knowledge. For example, a recent widow may need to learn to handle the household finances when there is no one else around to do it for her. Although she may not be excited about learning how to pay monthly bills or balance a checkbook, she needs to learn how to do it and therefore has a very strong motivation. Personal motivation is a strong predictor of whether older adults are capable of learning.

Memory is another important factor in an older adult's ability to learn. If new information is not processed from sensory reception through working memory and stored in secondary memory, learning has not occurred. If an older adult has difficulty hearing the instructions or seeing visual materials, new information becomes more difficult to learn. Older adults also learn at a slower rate than young people. Too much information

Table 3.1	**Psychological System Age-Related Changes**	
Intelligence	General levels of intelligence are usually consistent over the life course with adequate nutrition and hydration. In absence of disease, crystallized intelligence (general knowledge) increases while fluid intelligence (problem-solving) may decrease under time constraints.	
Personality	Personality remains relatively consistent over the life course but there is always the ability to grow and change. Older adults are still challenged by a variety of psychosocial tasks important to personal and emotional satisfaction. Older adults may react to stress of any sort with a stronger emotional and physical response.	
Memory	Sensory memory remains strong and may stimulate long-term memory, which remains intact in the absence of disease. Short-term memory (primary memory) may be more difficult unless there is a strong motivation to remember. Accessing both short- and long-term memory may take longer.	
Learning	Older adults remain very capable of continuing to learn if they find the learning relevant to their own lives. Learning is enhanced by good environmental conditions such as adequate light and sound.	

presented too quickly simply cannot be processed by the older mind and therefore will not be processed into secondary memory (Table 3.1).

Older Adults and Sexuality

An essential component of psychosocial well-being in older adults is their interest in and ability to express their sexuality, regardless of physical or mental health. The significance of sexuality goes beyond the discussion of reproductive issues and the dangers of sexually transmitted diseases. Throughout the life cycle, the ability to experience warmth, caring, physical intimacy, and connection to significant others contributes to an adult's self-esteem. Sexual activity may also take the form of masturbation for older adults who do not, or choose not to, have a partner. The significance of an older adult's sexuality is entirely dependent on what it means to the individual older adult. Being sexually active or inactive is not an issue of normal or dysfunctional behavior as defined by the social worker but as experienced by the older adult (Styrcula, 2001).

As emphasized in Chapter 2 in the discussion of the growing number of elders who are HIV positive, there is a tendency for physical and mental health professionals to avoid discussing sexuality and sexual activity with older adults based on the false assumption that older adults are not sexually active. The National Social Life, Health, and Aging Project (NSHAP), the largest study of its kind focused specifically on older adults, found that 53 percent of respondents between the ages of 65 and 74 years and 26 percent of respondents between the ages of 75 and 85 reported sexual activity within the previous 12 months (Lindau et al., 2007). The most sexually active older adults over age 65 were those who were married (both men and women) and reported their health as very good or excellent, suggesting that one's physical and mental health are crucial not only to the ability to engage in sex but also to maintain interest in sexual activity.

The prevalence of continuing sexual activity among older adults will likely increase as baby boomers grow older. Baby boomers reached adulthood at a time when safe, effective contraceptive methods became widely available, thereby encouraging earlier and more frequent sexual activity. Sexual activity became less connected to reproductive activities and more strongly associated with self-expression and physical pleasure. A more liberated attitude about sex and an increase in the life expectancy of both men and women suggest older adult sexuality will become a more salient issue for physical and mental health providers (Kingsberg, 2000).

Factors Affecting Sexual Activity in Older Adults

The kind and frequency of sexual activity among older adults (Kamel, 2001) is contingent on both physical and psychosocial factors. Two physical conditions, in particular, account for much of the loss of ability to perform or interest in sexual activity among older adults. For men, *erectile dysfunction*, or the inability to achieve or maintain an erection, may make sexual intercourse frustrating, embarrassing, or physically impossible (Lindau et al., 2007). Regular or occasional erectile dysfunction affects 50 percent of men in their 50s and up to 70 percent of men in their 70s (Styrcula, 2001). In the NSHAP study, 37 percent of men reported erectile difficulties, but only 14 percent of respondents reported using medication to improve sexual function. Medication such as Viagra has shown great promise in decreasing the incidence of erectile dysfunction, but older men may be uncomfortable seeking a prescription for the drug. Twenty-five percent of male respondents in the NSHAP study reported that they avoided sexual activity completely as a way to deal with performance problems, some indication of the assault on an older man's self-esteem caused by this condition.

For women, dyspareunia, painful intercourse due to vaginal atrophy or lack of lubrication following menopause, may serve as a deterrent to any interest in sexual intercourse, especially if one has not been sexually active on an ongoing basis. Synthetic estrogen and lubrication gels have been found to be very effective in treating this condition, but older women have to know they are available and be willing to use them (Gelfand, 2000; Styrcula, 2001). The physical discomfort during sex associated with sexual inactivity is often referred to as widow or widower syndrome, because it most often appears in older adults who have been without a regular sexual partner for an extended period of time (Capuzzi & Friel, 1990). Almost one-third of women in the NSHAP study indicated they avoided sex completely due to physical discomfort (Lindau et al., 2007).

Frail physical or mental health often accounts for the decline in sexual activity among older adults, even if they remain interested in expressing their sexuality. Cardiovascular diseases, diabetes, and orthopedic limitations, such as severe arthritis, joint replacement, or osteoporosis, may prevent an older adult from physically engaging in sexual relations safely or comfortably. Side effects of medications used to treat common chronic health conditions may seriously impair sexual functioning or responsiveness as well. Even though many older adults retain a desire to continue or initiate sexual activity, an acceptable partner may not be available (Kingsberg, 2000; Lindau et al., 2007; Walker & Ephross, 1999). With the uneven ratio of older men to older women, men may have multiple opportunities for sexual partners, whereas women may have very few. Women were less likely to report sexual activity than men, with the most frequent reason being the lack of a partner, consistent with the tendency of women to live longer than their partners (Lindau et al., 2007). Older men are more likely to be married, and older women are more likely to be widowed, thus affecting the opportunities for sexual expression in an ongoing, intimate relationship.

Perhaps the most significant factors affecting an older adult's level of sexual activity are attitudes (including the attitudes of the older adult), adult children, and physical and mental health-care providers (Capuzzi & Friel, 1990; Schlesinger, 1996). Some older adults retain a strong interest in remaining sexually active and would identify themselves as having a healthy libido and no apparent obstacles to continuing regular and satisfying sexual intercourse. These are not the older adults who come to the attention of either physical or mental health professionals. Another group of older adults remains interested in sexual activity but faces problems with erectile dysfunction or painful intercourse as previously described. These older adults, if interested, need to be made aware of and given access to drug or hormone therapies that can restore normal sexual functioning in an atmosphere that respects their self-determination and dignity. In the NSHAP study, 38 percent of men and 22 percent of women reported having discussed sex with their physicians since they turned age 50, but the statistics suggest that even more older adults could benefit from medical intervention if given the opportunity (Lindau et al., 2007). The third group of older adults may simply no longer be interested in sexual activity due to any of the reasons discussed previously or because it is simply no longer an important issue to them. It is sound ethical professional practice to respect this decision by an older adult without judgment. Any intervention to enhance an older adult's sexual performance or libido should be considered only if an older adult expresses dissatisfaction with his or her current status (Styrcula, 2001).

Intimacy

Whether sexually active or not, older adults have a continuing need for intimacy—a strong emotional connection to at least one other person. This may or may not be achieved within the context of a relationship with a spouse or partner. Some couples remain together out of habit and familiarity, rather than out of a deep sense of love and commitment to each other. Their intimacy needs may not be met by their partners but may be met by deep friendships or connections to family members. It is common among older women that intimacy needs are met by women friends with whom they develop interdependent relationships to cope with widowhood and the lack of family located close to them. This pattern represents a consistent way of women defining themselves and getting their psychosocial needs met. Relational theory proposes that females, from the time of birth, develop within the context of relationships with parents, siblings, friends, and partners, whereas males are more likely to develop a strong sense of independence and individuality, which requires some level of separation from the same relationships that facilitate female development (Golden, 1996). This theory does suggest that older women, as opposed to men, may find it easier to develop and keep close friendships throughout the life cycle and turn to those relationships to meet intimacy needs.

Lakritz and Knoblauch (1999) found that many of the older adults they studied defined love and intimacy in more global terms than deeply meaningful relationships with other persons. Older adults identified their experiences in coping with loss and suffering combined with their vision of hope for their grown children and growing grandchildren as an expression of love and intimacy. They cited deeply satisfying life work and play activities, a sense of connection to friends and family members, and strong sociopolitical convictions as the sources of their sense of well-being and fulfillment with their lives.

Sexuality and Institutionalized Older Adults

Providing older adults in assisted living and nursing homes an opportunity to express their sexuality presents a special challenge to physical and mental health providers. Older adults may continue to express interest in sexual activities, with varying degrees of appropriateness, even in the later stages of dementia or debilitating illness. Many of the questions raised by sexual expression in institutions have to do with the ability of an older adult to make an informed decision about his or her own sexual activity (Kuhn, 2002; Reingold & Burros, 2004). Although clearly protecting both the older adult from physical danger and ridicule and other vulnerable older adults from exploitation in this setting is most important, staff and family members need to approach an older adult's continuing sexual interest with sensitivity and compassion. Sexual interest is an expression of a continuing need for love and intimacy. Institutional staff should be trained with better knowledge in this area, and a sexual history and assessment should be included in the care plan for older adults when relevant (Kamel, 2001; Kuhn, 2002; Reingold & Burros, 2004). Residents should be given ample opportunity to socialize as much as possible with other residents to meet the needs for social interaction and stimulation. When a sexual relationship with another adult is not practical or possible, Kamel (2001) has recommended that family and friends offer more physical affection through kissing and hugging to meet the older adult's continuing needs for affection.

However, there are circumstances when open sexual expression in an institution is not appropriate. In situations such as public masturbation or inappropriate sexual advances toward more vulnerable residents, it is necessary for staff and family members to intervene. For older adults with good cognitive awareness, directly addressing the appropriateness of the behavior is necessary. In the absence of cognitive limitations, older adults are perfectly capable of stopping offensive behavior if staff and family members make it clear that the behavior will not be tolerated. If an older adult has some degree of dementia, it may be effective to verbally or physically redirect the behavior through distracting the older adult or isolating the older adult from the offended gender until the behavior stops (Kamel, 2001). If an older adult is prone to exposing himself or herself to others in public, clothing that opens in the back, thus making it harder to remove or open, combined with a direct care provider of the same gender, may make it more difficult for the older adult to engage in the inappropriate behavior. All these suggestions preserve the older adult's dignity and protect other vulnerable older adults.

SOCIAL THEORIES OF AGING

In the discussion about the psychological changes that accompany aging, it is clear that even though psychological changes occur on an individual basis, this change is deeply influenced by the social environment of the older adult. This section of the chapter will present a number of different social theories of aging, descriptions of various ways social scientists have speculated or observed that older adults adapt to the aging process in relationship to their social environment. These theories fall roughly into two schools of thought. First are what are known as "prescriptive theories," which attempt to explain how older adults and social structures can "successfully" accommodate the presence of older adults and aging as a process. These theories are early attempts to discern where aging and older adults "fit" in the greater social context. The second set of theories are known as "descriptive," which attempts to simply describe the commonalities that diverse populations exhibit in the process of aging, but not to evaluate what is "successful." Descriptive theories are heavily influenced by the postmodern school of social constructionism, which postulates that older adults experience "different worlds in aging" (Kolb, 2004) and that the aging experience is quite different for lesbian, gay, bisexual, or transgendered (LGBT) older adults and older adults of color.

Prescriptive Social Theories of Aging

Role Theory

One of the earliest attempts to explain how older adults adjust to aging as a social role is role theory (Cavan, Burgess, Havighurst, & Goldhammer, 1949; Phillips, 1957). This theory focuses on the behavior and insight of the individual older adult rather than viewing the aging process as significantly affected by socioenvironmental factors. Roles are sets of expected behavior patterns defined by an individual's relationship to another person or social institution. For example, the role of parent is defined by the relationship to a child. The role of student is defined by the relationship to an institution of higher learning or a professor. Role theory postulates that life is a series of sequentially defined roles. The quality of an older adult's adjustment to the later years is dependent on the ability to move from roles identified with youth and middle age to those associated with aging. Roles associated with middle age may be parent, worker, spouse, and active community member. For an older adult, these roles may change to age-related roles, such as grandparent, retiree, and widow. Older adults lose some roles from middle age and gain new ones. One's personal self-esteem and social identity are deeply embedded in these social roles. According to role theory, older adults demonstrate successful aging when they can move from one set of roles to those appropriate to their age norms. Dissatisfaction with the aging process develops when people are unable to make this shift or cannot identify new roles to replace old ones (Havighurst & Albrecht, 1953).

Disengagement and Activity Theories

Disengagement theory was proposed to shift the emphasis away from the individual to a focus on the "function" of aging for society. Aging occurs within a greater social context. Therefore, to understand aging, one must look at it in relationship to younger persons. Disengagement theory proposes that a mutual disengagement by both society and the individual occurs as social and political power transfers from one generation to another (Cumming & Henry, 1961). Adaptive aging occurs when older adults disengage from active roles in society to more passive roles to make room for the development of new leadership among younger people. This theory emphasizes the adaptive nature of this mutual disengagement. It does not necessarily imply that older adults are happy with this process, but merely that it is adaptive. Ultimately, disengagement serves the best interests of both the individual and society according to this theory.

Disengagement theory has come under extensive criticism both scientifically and anecdotally. The idea that withdrawing from society is adaptive seems to contradict what professionals know about people staying active physically and intellectually. As social workers, it would leave us wondering what activities would be deemed appropriate for older adults. As the sociological and psychological community has learned more about the social process of aging, the validity of disengagement theory as the sole explanation for the function of aging in society has been discounted. This does not mean that the pattern of disengagement is not seen in some older adults, but rather that it is an individual adjustment to aging, not a universally accepted or recommended pattern of behavior.

Activity theory offers the opposite of what is proposed by disengagement theory as a model for successful aging. Activity theory predicts that older adults who maintain active and reciprocal relationships with their social environment are those most likely to age successfully (Maddox, 1966; Spence, 1975). Older adults who travel, work part-time, or participate in a wide range of social activities find old age a rewarding and satisfying time in their lives. If older adults withdraw from social activities, they are more likely to become depressed and dissatisfied with old age. In theory, few would disagree that purposeful activity for older adults contributes to a greater sense of attachment to the social environment and the opportunity for greater personal rewards. Every young person hopes the retirement years will be filled with lots of exciting new adventures. Activity theory, however, fails to account for the physical health problems and socioeconomic limitations that preclude older adults' active participation in society (Fry, 1992; Lynott & Lynott, 1996). Although this theory is still considered as an ideal in adjustment to aging, it is rightfully accused of being oblivious to the realities that older adults of color or older adults with disabilities face.

Continuity Theory

Continuity theory states that older adults and society fare best when older adults continue a consistent level of activity throughout their lives but also develop an "adaptive capacity" to reflect changes in health and socioeconomic circumstances (Atchley, 2000). Contrary to other social theories, older adults do not develop a totally new way of approaching their lives as they age. Rather, old age is a continuation of all lifelong activity patterns adapted as necessary over time. Older adults are most satisfied when they maintain a mature, integrated personality consistent with previous patterns of activity. If people have led an active, socially engaged life in middle age, they will be happiest when they can continue to do so in old age. If an individual has led a minimally active life as an adult, this pattern will persist into old age. Older adults are simply more of what they were when they were younger, according to this theory. Intuitively, this theory makes sense and is consistent with what psychology says about the stability of basic personality characteristics over the life span. It is also consistent with social work's commitment to the belief that people can change and adapt as necessary. It reinforces the concept of personality as both structure and process.

The major criticism of this theory, however, is that it fails to account for unanticipated changes in both physical health and social circumstances (Fry, 1992). For example, if a woman has been athletic most of her life and suddenly faces restrictions in physical activity due to the dangers imposed by osteoporosis, does this mean she will not make a satisfactory adjustment to aging and is destined to be unhappy? If an older man has had few friends throughout his life due to family and job responsibilities, does this mean he probably will never be able to develop new social ties as a retired widower? The criticism of the continuity theory is that it is a very restricted way of thinking about the potential for change among older adults as they adapt to new circumstances that will likely accompany the aging process.

Prescriptive theories of aging were social theorists' first attempts to describe how society and its older adults could get aging "right." If society knew whether to hold on or let go of its older adults and older adults knew whether to stay connected or go away, maybe the challenges of a population whose social function is still not clear (even to this day) would resolve themselves. These theories have been appropriately criticized for looking at aging as a unidimensional and fixed process, rather than as the dynamic, multidimensional phenomenon as it has come to be understood. By presenting optimal aging as a fixed process, these theories have also been faulted for not recognizing the unique experiences of LGBT older adults and those of color whose experiences of growing old and being old are much different. Descriptive social theories of aging attempt to be more multidimensional in developing an understanding of the aging experience.

Descriptive Social Theories of Aging

Social Constructionism

Social constructionism moves beyond the restrictive perspectives of role, activity, disengagement, and continuity theories by proposing that people of all ages participate in everyday life on the basis of the social meanings they have created for themselves (Ray, 1996). There is no such thing as a "fixed reality" that exists for all individuals. People create their own realities, and these realities shift over time. A young man may see his world as one in which his responsibility is to his job and his family. His view of the world prioritizes his activities and his attitudes. A young mother may feel her first responsibility is to her children and order her activities to reflect that view. However, when both men and women reach their later years, their social construction of the reality of their world changes. Having raised their children, their priorities may shift away from parenting as a top priority to a renewed focus on being a couple or to participating in activities that focus more on personal rewards than fulfilling responsibilities to others. The reality people construct for their own lives explains how they behave. If older adults see late life as a time for less social, more introspective activities, that is what they will do. If older adults see late life as a time for doing all the things they did not have time for earlier in life, they are more likely to pursue a more activities-oriented life. This theory does not necessarily see any particular orientation to old age as either functional or dysfunctional, healthy or pathological, but rather a reflection of the individual's perception of this stage in life.

Social constructionists are less focused on adaptation patterns and more interested in how people define these experiences for themselves. Using qualitative methods, such as personal interviews and narratives, social scientists gather information about what social clues older adults use to define the reality of old age. One older woman may see widowhood as a new opportunity for self-development; another may see this same event as the beginning of the wait for her own death, with much to be feared and little to be enjoyed. One older man may retire to the couch to simply enjoy doing nothing; another may welcome the lack of job-related activities to take up active leisure pursuits such as golf or tennis. Social constructionism views aging and its subsequent adjustment as a uniquely individual process dictated by each individual's own social perceptions. If people construct their own social realities in old age, the gerontological social worker is challenged to try to understand what that reality is for older adults. Understanding how people perceive the world in which they function helps the social worker to help older adults participate in activities and interventions consistent with their worldviews.

Friend (1991) expands the understanding of the aging experience through the social constructionism lens as it applies to LGBT older adults. LGBT older adults create meaning of what it means to be lesbian, gay, bisexual, or transgendered from messages in the context of social norms. The sociohistorical context in which they grew up creates their own cognitive and behavioral acceptance (or lack of) based on societal messages about heterosexuality as the norm. Those older adults who internalized the negative social images of nontraditional sexual orientation will logically have greater levels of self-hatred, low self-esteem, or minimal self-acceptance, factors likely to result in poorer mental health and social integration. Those LGBT adults who have felt affirmed in their sexual orientation and constructed positive attributes of their sexuality will be much better prepared for the challenges that accompany the aging process. They are most likely to have developed stronger social support systems and a more integrated psychological self. The experience of being LGBT will be deeply influenced by the power of internalized messages, thus explaining why the aging experience will be so dramatically different for LGBT older adults.

The Person-Environment Perspective

Consistent with social work's emphasis on the importance of understanding human behavior in the social environment is the person-environment perspective offered by environmental gerontologists. Environmental gerontologists propose that successful and rewarding aging is contingent on the ability of an older adult to manage the constraints and opportunities of the physical-social environment (Wahl & Oswald, 2010). Older adults thrive on a sense of belonging in their physical environment and need to feel their immediate living environment is comfortable, safe, and familiar and to which they feel they belong, a "place" not just a "space" (Wahl & Oswald, 2010). Older adults may have a strong social bond with their homes as a place filled with memories and experiences that are a source of satisfaction and happiness for them. *Home* means much more than a place to live. Environmental gerontologists describe this phenomenon as "person-environment belonging," which is not unique to older adults but plays a more important role to individuals as they grow older and face the challenge of maintaining their dignity and independence.

However, this need to belong must be balanced with the ability to adapt that environment as needed to accommodate the physical and functional changes that accompany the aging process. This is known as "person-environment agency." *Agency* in this context means the need and ability to be proactive in modifying one's environment as necessary. How well older adults can adapt to their existing environment, adapt that environment, or change to a different environment in light of changing functional needs determines how well older adults adapt to the aging process. It is the interaction between the need to belong to a living environment and a proactive response to adapting that environment that presents one of the most significant challenges of being an older adult. For some older adults, aging in their own homes with some physical adaptations or support services is a realistic option. They have balanced the need for belonging with agency. For others, staying in a lifelong home is neither realistic nor desirable. Moving to an apartment or assisted-living facility can provide a more satisfactory balance between a safe comfortable place to live and access to needed services and support. This adaptation can also achieve a balance between belonging and agency. The degree of dissonance an older adult experiences between these two person-environmental needs can be a powerful predictor of how well individuals handle the challenges and rewards later in life.

This theoretical perspective is especially valuable to social workers who often struggle with an older adult's choice to stay in a house that has become too much work or too expensive to maintain but has deep meaning as "home." Even when a more supportive arrangement such as an apartment may seem a simple, logical choice to family members, the psychological and emotional attachment to a family home exerts a powerful influence on an older adult's decision to move or not move. It is a challenge to the social worker as well to help an older adult find the best balance between belonging and agency, the ability to remain as proactive as possible in mastering his or her environment.

Gender, Race and Ethnicity, Class, and the Life Course

One of the major criticisms of social theories of aging is that they are insensitive to the unique experiences of older adults who fall outside a traditional white, middle-class male experience of growing older. Stoller and Gibson (2000) offer a life course perspective on aging that introduces the elements of personal biography, sociocultural factors, and sociocultural issues and the effect these factors have on the unique experiences people face in the aging process. They propose that there are discernible patterns in the experiences of different segments of the population, such as persons of color, women, LGBT older adults, and those of lower socioeconomic groups. Membership in these groups defines an individual's sense of self as being different and affects opportunities available to them throughout their entire lives. The effect of lifelong discrimination, limited access to adequate education, employment, and health care increase the chances of facing considerable challenges as an older adult. To identify whether an older adult has "aged successfully" without acknowledging the obstacles they have faced is to devalue not only the older adult but also the ways in which they have coped with ascribed disadvantages. Therefore, aging in the social context cannot be truly understood or appreciated without a deep sensitivity to the experience of diversity. This perspective is especially helpful to social work in that it should help the practitioner listen to these unique life experiences in the process of designing interventions. This requires the practitioner to capitalize on the strengths an older adult has used to cope with a lifetime of challenges and obstacles but also recognize that failing health and poverty are not the exclusive products of poor choices in an individual's life.

"SUCCESSFUL" PSYCHOSOCIAL AGING

In addition to studying the factors that contribute to the maintenance of good physical health in old age discussed in Chapter 2, both the MacArthur Study and the Harvard Study of Adult Development examined the psychosocial factors that contribute to successful aging. In general, both studies confirmed what gerontologists have long assumed: cognitive and intellectual decline among older adults is the exception to the rule. It also confirms that a strong social support network is one of the most important predictors of good psychosocial adjustment to aging.

Cognitive and Intellectual Functioning

Much of the functional loss older adults fear as they grow older is preventable, according to the MacArthur Study. Although older adults do experience very real changes in short-term memory as they age, severe memory loss is not common or inevitable in old age. For older adults who have lost some of their memory function, a variety of mental exercises and a concentrated effort to retrain memory can result in almost complete recovery of memory function (Rowe & Kahn, 1998). Those older adults studied who retained strong cognitive and intellectual capabilities made an active effort to use their intellectual resources every single day. They continued to do crossword puzzles, play other word games, read the paper, or find other ways to challenge their minds. Exercising the mind is similar to exercising the body—use it or lose it!

Valliant (2002) also identified the attainment of wisdom as a crucial factor in maintaining healthy intellectual and cognitive functioning later in life. He defines wisdom as "the capacity and the willingness to step back from the immediacy of the moment—whether it is an affect, a judgment, or a conflict—in order to attain perspective" (Valliant, 2002, p. 251). This pertained to all socioeconomic groups within the study, not just the well-educated participants. Having the ability to process what one has learned in life and gain a perspective about what is important (and what is not) helped older adults to remain inquisitive about their surroundings and keep a positive attitude about their own abilities to handle what life dealt them.

It is not clear whether good mental functioning produced this personal self-confidence or whether the self-confidence produced good mental functioning, but the two factors appear to be strongly related. It is important that older adults still see themselves as masters of their own fates, even when faced with physical changes associated with aging or other changes in their social systems.

The Significance of Social Support

Social support is one of the most important predictors of satisfaction and emotional well-being among older adults, a finding confirmed by both the MacArthur Study and the Harvard Study of Adult Development. Rowe and Kahn (1998) found that social support plays an important role in buffering the deleterious effects of all kinds of losses that face older adults. Those older adults described as successfully aging were often those who survived and thrived because they remained deeply engaged with family, friends, and productive activity (Rowe & Kahn, 1998). Having the support of family and friends can help a widowed older adult face the array of new challenges that accompany a new life without his or her spouse or partner. Losing a significant, lifelong friend can be devastating to an older adult, but it may be less painful if his or her remaining friends can offer emotional support during bereavement. Valliant (2002) added an important concept to the understanding of the importance of social support to older adults—generativity. Generativity is defined as feeling a sense of responsibility for the well-being of the next generation through physically and emotionally caring for younger people. Older adults who nurture their relationships with grandchildren, nieces and nephews, or other young people had something to do and someone who cared about them. These older adults were able to identify what was important to them in their lives, who cared about them, and what activities helped them to maintain a positive self-image.

Social isolation was found to be a powerful risk factor not only for the development of cognitive and intellectual decline but also for physical illness as well (Rowe & Kahn, 1998). It is somewhat difficult, however, to determine whether individuals with better health have better social support systems or whether better social support systems actually determine better health (Valliant, 2002). Older adults with concerned family or friends are more likely to attend to physical health issues as others encourage them to see a health-care provider regularly and help facilitate these medical visits. Knowing that others are concerned about an older adult's health and are paying attention may actually encourage older adults to be more diligent about maintaining medication schedules or following treatment plans.

IMPLICATIONS OF PSYCHOSOCIAL CHANGES FOR SOCIAL WORK PRACTICE WITH OLDER ADULTS

The findings of the MacArthur Study and the Harvard Study of Adult Development on the psychosocial changes associated with the aging process are very encouraging in terms of identifying what older adults and helping professionals can do to help make this time in life a positive and rewarding experience for older adults. Getting older does not inherently mean the loss of memory, cognitive abilities, or intellectual functioning. Nor does getting older mean that older adults must face disengaging from the world around them. These findings suggest a number of important implications for gerontological social work practice and ways in which helping professionals can provide opportunities for older adults to maximize their psychosocial functioning.

Provide Opportunities but Respect Choice

Older adults who continue to challenge their minds and keep their intellectual curiosity alive tend to retain their cognitive abilities longer. Providing opportunities for older adults of all income levels to continue to learn through adult education programs, social and cultural experiences, and the acquisition of new skills is an essential part of successful aging. Making sure that obstacles created by lack of financial resources, physical barriers such as lack of transportation or handicapped accessibility, or simple lack of knowledge about the existence of such opportunities do not limit learning opportunities for older adults is an important role for social workers. Do older adults know about educational programs or learning opportunities? Can they access those resources? Are these opportunities of interest to an older adult? If the answer to all these questions is "yes," what can the social worker do to help an older adult connect to these services?

One of the most frustrating aspects of working with older adults in many settings—especially nursing homes, adult day health centers, and congregate living centers—is developing educational programming and then finding older adults are not interested in participating. It is hard to hear older adults complain about not having anything to do and then discover they rarely participate in what does exist in these settings. If removing obstacles and providing ongoing support does not result in an older adult's participation, it may be necessary simply to respect the older adult's decision not to participate. Even though the social worker can be convinced that this is just what the older adult needs, the profession's commitment to self-determination requires that the older adult's choice be honored.

Everything Takes More Time

In the absence of disease, older adults retain the ability to perform complex tasks or remember important information if they are given more time. Under the pressures of large caseloads and the time restrictions of managed care, it is easy for a social worker to rush through the assessment process or become frustrated when it is necessary to take extended periods of time to explain medication regimens and complicated appointment schedules. Slow down! Give the older adult time to process what is being said. If need be, explain the same information in a variety of ways to reinforce the information. Adults learn best when they see the relevance of the information for their own lives and are active participants in the process. Rushing older adults can make them very resistant.

Psychosocial Health Is Often Contingent on Physical Health

The quality of an older adult's psychosocial functioning is highly contingent on the quality of his or her physical health. If an older adult is plagued by physical complaints and generally does not feel well, focusing on opportunities to enhance social contact or stimulate his or her intellectual abilities may prove futile. This statement is qualified, however, by the importance of recognizing that older adults often somatize emotional problems, making it difficult to tell what is actually an emotional problem and what is a legitimate physical complaint. Therefore, in recognition of the biopsychosocial approach supported by the profession, it is important that older adults have access to health care and be carefully monitored by a physician while the social worker is addressing psychosocial issues. The extensive coverage of the biological aspects of the aging process in Chapter 2 was presented explicitly for this reason. The biological changes of aging both enhance and detract from an older adult's psychosocial adjustment to this life stage.

Social Isolation Can Be Deadly for Older Adults

The danger of social isolation for older adults and the ways in which it contributes to depression, dementia, substance abuse, and older adult abuse is a dominant theme in this book. Older adults need to stay connected to someone or something for good psychosocial health. For some older adults, this connection is with family and friends. For others, a beloved pet, phone friends, Internet chat rooms, or even plants can fulfill the need to stay connected. Older adults need social interaction of some kind to maintain both intellectual and social functioning. It is not only the sense of social interaction with others that is important to older adults but also the sense of being productive and useful, however an older adult defines it. For some older adults, productivity is as obvious as volunteering in a community agency or school. For others, it may be defined more subtly in the form of gardening, playing cards, taking care of grandchildren, keeping their homes tidy, or surfing the Internet. It is most important that older adults define the activity as productive for themselves, not as compared to anyone else's judgment.

Change Is Always Possible

Although the continuity theory suggests that older adults' adaptations to aging are often continuations of lifetime behavior patterns, it is always possible for older adults to change their activity patterns. Believing that people can change is a fundamental underpinning of the social work profession. The older woman who never completed high school and spent her entire life concerned with taking care of her family may be an excellent candidate for taking a course at a local community college. Never having had the opportunity earlier in life to participate in some activities is not an accurate indication that an older adult would not be interested now. Likewise, an older man who has never even been outside his hometown may be an enthusiastic convert to bus trips or other travel opportunities. Old age as a time in the life course offers endless opportunities for older adults to change and try new things. Although continuity theory may provide an important insight into anticipating how any given individual may adjust to old age, it is not a life sentence. The range of new activities an older adult may be willing to try may be limited only by the creativity and encouragement of the social worker.

SUMMARY

Contrary to popular belief, a deterioration of cognitive and intellectual functioning is not inevitable in old age. Older adults actually have more crystallized intelligence than their younger counterparts, reflecting a lifetime of learning and living. The speed at which an individual is able to perform complex problem solving, known as fluid intelligence, however, does slow down as an individual ages, due to changes in the efficiency of the neurotransmitters in the brain. In the absence of any organic brain damage, such as that caused by Alzheimer's disease, depression, or poor nutrition, older adults retain the ability to learn new skills and remain active intellectually. Keeping the brain stimulated and engaged is essential to preserving these cognitive abilities.

Regardless of physical or mental health, an older adult's sexuality continues to be an important part of his or her psychosocial functioning. Physical illness or disability and the lack of a partner may change the way in which sexuality is expressed, but the need for intimacy and connection remains crucial throughout the life cycle. Difficulty in articulating their continued interest in sex and unintentional (or intentional) barriers in institutional settings combined with the attitudes of family and professionals may make expressing that sexuality frustrating for older adults.

An older adult's adaptation to the social context of aging depends on personal attitudes, the presence of a social support network, and the environmental context in which the older adult grows older. Some older adults continue to be active and engaged in their immediate social settings, substituting new and exciting activities for those in which they no longer can participate. Others withdraw to a more isolated life by choice or chance. These older adults may view their later years as a time to move away from the demands of middle age and take it easy. Still other older adults find a way to combine a more modest level of activity with time to relax and enjoy leisure. There is no single "successful" way to adapt socially to aging.

References

Atchley, R. C. (2000). *The social forces in later life*. Belmont, CA: Wadsworth.
Capuzzi, D., & Friel, S. E. (1990). Current trends in sexuality and aging: An update for counselors. *Journal of Mental Health Counseling, 12*(3), 342–353.

Cavan, R. S., Burgess, E. W., Havighurst, R. J., & Goldhammer, H. (1949). *Personal adjustment in old age*. Chicago: Science Research Associates.

Craik, F. I. M. (2000). Age-related changes in human memory. In D. Park & Schwarz, N. (Eds.), *Cognitive aging: A primer* (pp. 75–92). Philadelphia: Psychology Press.

Craik, F. I. M., & Jennings, J. M. (1992). Human memory. In F. I. M. Craik & T. A. Salthouse (Eds.), *The handbook of aging and cognition* (pp. 51–110). Hillsdale, NJ: Erlbaum.

Cumming, E., & Henry, W. E. (1961). *Growing old: The process of disengagement*. New York: Basic Books.

Erikson, E. (1963). *Childhood and society* (2nd ed.). New York: Norton.

Friend, R. M. (1991). Older lesbian and gay people: A theory of successful aging. *Journal of Homosexuality*, *20*, 99–118.

Fry, P. S. (1992). Major social theories of aging and their implications for counseling concepts and practice: A cultural review. *The Counseling Psychologist, 20*(2), 246–329.

Gelfand, M. M. (2000). Sexuality among older women. *Journal of Women's Health and Gender-Based Medicine, 9*(Supplement 1), S15–S20.

Golden, C. (1996). Relational theories of white women's development. In J. Chrisler, C. Golden, & P. Rozee (Eds.), *Lectures on the psychology of women* (pp. 229–242). New York: McGraw-Hill.

Havighurst, R. J., & Albrecht, R. (1953). *Older people*. New York: Longmans, Green.

Hawley, K. S., Cherry, K. E., Sum L. J., Chiu, Y. W., & Jazwinski, S. M. (2006). Knowledge of memory aging in adulthood. *International Journal of Aging and Human Development, 63*(4), 317–334.

Kamel, H. K. (2001). Sexuality in aging: Focus on institutionalized elderly. *Annals of Long-Term Care, 9*(5), 64–72.

Kingsberg, S. A. (2000). The psychological impact of aging on sexuality and relationships. *Journal of Women's Health and Gender-Based Medicine, 9*(Supplement 1), S33–S38.

Kolb, P. J. (2004). Theories of aging and social work practice with sensitivity to diversity: Are there useful theories? *Journal of Human Behavior in the Social Environment, 9*(4), 3–24.

Kuhn, D. (2002). Intimacy, sexuality and residents with dementia. *Alzheimer's Care Quarterly, 3*(2), 165–176.

Lakritz, K. R., & Knoblauch, T. M. (1999). Older adults on love: Dialogues on the consciousness, cultivation, and expression of love. New York: Parabola.

Lazarus, R. S., & Cohen, J. B. (1977). *The hassles scale, stress and coping project*. Berkeley: University of California.

Leventhal, H., Rabin, C., Levanthal, E. A., & Burns, E. (2001). Health risk behaviors and aging. In J. E. Birren & K. W. Schaie (Eds.), *Handbook of the psychology of aging* (pp. 186–214). San Diego, CA: Academic Press.

Lindau, S. T., Schumm, L. P., Laumann, E. O., Levinson, W., Muirchearaigh, C. A., & Waite, L. J. (2007). A study of sexuality and health among older adults in the United States. *New England Journal of Medicine, 357*(8), 762–774.

Lynott, R. J., & Lynott, P. P. (1996). Tracing the course of theoretical development in the sociology of aging. *The Gerontologist, 36*(6), 749–760.

Maddox, G. L. (1966). Persistence in life-style among the elderly. *Proceedings on the Seventh International Congress of Gerontology, 6*, 309–311.

Menniger, W. W. (1999). Adaptational challenges and coping in late life. *Bulletin of the Menniger Clinic, 63*(2), A4–A15.

Monopoli, J., Vaccaro, F., Christmann, E., & Badgett, J. (2000). Personality as a predictor of depression among the elderly. *Clinical Gerontologist, 21*(3), 49–63.

Phillips, B. S. (1957). A role theory approach to adjustment in old age. *American Sociological Review, 22*, 212–217.

Ray, R. E. (1996). A postmodern perspective on feminist gerontology. *The Gerontologist, 36*, 674–680.

Reingold, D., & Burros, N. (2004). Sexuality in the nursing home. *Journal of Gerontological Social Work, 43*(2/3), 175–186.

Rowe, J. W., & Kahn, R. L. (1998). *Successful aging*. New York: Pantheon.

Rozencwajg, P., Cherfi, M., Ferrandez, A. M., Lautry, J., Lemoine, C. & Loarer, E. (2005). Age related differences in the strategies used by middle aged adults to solve a block design task. *International Journal of Aging and Human Development, 60*(2), 159–182.

Ruth, J. E., & Coleman, P. (1996). Personality and aging: Coping and management of the self in later life. In J. E. Birren & K. W. Schaie (Eds.), *Handbook of the psychology of aging* (4th ed., pp. 308–322). San Diego, CA: Academic.

Ryff, C. D., Kwan, C. M. L., & Singer, B. H. (2001). Personality and aging: Flourishing agendas and future challenges. In J. E. Birren & K. W. Schaie (Eds.), *Handbook of the psychology of aging* (pp. 477–499). San Diego, CA: Academic Press.

Salthouse, T. A. (2000). Pressing issues in cognitive aging. In D. Park & N. Schwarz (Eds.), *Cognitive aging: A primer* (43–54). Philadelphia, PA: Psychology Press.

Schaie, K. W. (1996). Intellectual development in adulthood. In J. E. Birren & K. W. Schaie (Eds.), *Handbook of the psychology of aging* (4th ed., pp. 266–286). San Diego, CA: Academic.

Schlesinger, B. (1996). The sexless years or sex rediscovered. *Journal of Gerontological Social Work, 26*(1/2), 117–131.

Smith, A. D. (1996). Memory. In J. E. Birren & K. W. Schaie (Eds.), *Handbook of the psychology of aging* (4th ed., pp. 236–250). San Diego, CA: Academic.

Snowdon, D. (2001). Aging with grace: What the nun study teaches us about leading longer, healthier and more meaningful lives. New York: Bantam Books.

Spence, D. R. (1975). The meaning of engagement. *International Journal of Aging and Human Development, 6*, 193–198.

Stoller, E., & Gibson, R. (2000). Advantages of using the life course framework in studying aging. In E. Stoller & R. Gibson (Eds.), *Worlds of difference: Inequality in the aging experience* (pp. 19–32). Thousand Oaks, CA: Pine Forge Press.

Styrcula, L. (2001). Under cover no more: Plain talk about mature sexuality. *Nursing Spectrum, 11*(12DC), 16–17.

Valliant, G. E. (2002). *Aging well.* New York: Little, Brown and Company.

Vella, J. (2000). Taking learning to task: Creative strategies for teaching adults. San Francisco: Jossey-Bass.

Wahl, H. W. (2001). Environmental influences on aging and behavior. In J. E. Birren & K. W. Schaie (Eds.), *Handbook of the psychology of aging* (pp. 215–240). San Diego, CA: Academic Press.

Wahl, H. W., & Oswald, F. (2010). Environmental perspectives on ageing. In D. Dannefer & C. Phillipson (Eds.), *The SAGE handbook of social gerontology* (pp. 111–124). Los Angeles, CA: Sage.

Waldstein, S. R. (2000). Health effects on the aging mind. In P. C. Stern & L. L. Carstensen (Eds.), *The aging mind: Opportunities in cognitive research* (pp. 189–217). Washington, DC: National Academy Press.

Waldstein, S. R. & Elias, M. F. (2000). *Neuropsychology of cardiovascular disease.* Mahwah, NJ: Erlbaum.

Walker, B. L., & Ephross, P. H. (1999). Knowledge and attitudes toward sexuality of a group of elderly. *Journal of Gerontological Social Work, 31*(1/2), 85–107.

Willis, S. L. (1996). Everyday problem solving. In J. E. Birren & K. W. Schaie (Eds.), *Handbook of the psychology of aging* (4th ed., pp. 287–307). San Diego, CA: Academic.

The following questions will test your application and analysis
of the content found within this chapter.

1. An older adult's memory is most affected by

   a. his or her physical health.

   b. opportunities to use and apply knowledge.

   c. his or her level of intelligence.

   d. how he or she copes with stress.

2. The factor(s) that most affect(s) an older adult's interest in sexual activity is (are)

   a. physical health.

   b. access to sexual partners.

   c. privacy and support in institutional settings.

   d. A combination of attitudes and physical health.

3. An older woman complains that she is lonely and depressed. Although she has family and friends nearby, she refuses to take the initiative to contact them and insists they should contact her first. What should the social worker do?

4. You are a supervisor of several young female social workers in a nursing home. These women have complained that an older male patient is engaging in highly sexually suggestive language when he talks to them. What should you do as their supervisor?

Conducting a Biopsychosocial Assessment

Competencies Applied with Practice Behaviors Examples —In This Chapter

- ❑ **Professional Identity**
- ☑ **Ethical Practice**
- ❑ **Critical Thinking**
- ☑ **Diversity in Practice**
- ❑ **Human Rights & Justice**
- ❑ **Research-Based Practice**
- ☑ **Human Behavior**
- ❑ **Policy Practice**
- ❑ **Practice Contexts**
- ☑ **Engage, Assess, Intervene, Evaluate**

AN ASSESSMENTS LOOK AT STRENGTHS AND CHALLENGES

In the preceding chapters, the spectrum of changes associated with biological, psychological, and social developments for older adults was discussed in detail. This knowledge serves as an important foundation in understanding changes older adults can expect in their lives as well as helping identify those conditions that are not part of the normal course of aging. Through a dynamic process of professional observation and input from the older adult being assessed, the social worker forms preliminary hypotheses about what interventions (if any) could help the older adult maximize his or her strengths to overcome the challenges faced as he or she grows older. The challenges faced by an older adult are the result of a complex interaction of the socioenvironmental context in which the older adult lives and the older adult's ability to grow and change as needed. It is tempting to see assessments as a way to primarily identify challenges but good assessments devote equal time to identifying the strengths and resilience older adults have used to solve a lifetime of other challenges. Having survived well into old age requires a sense of continuity, competence, and adaptability that suggests a wealth of resources that can be mobilized to meet the challenges that face older adults (Greene & Cohen, 2005).

A gerontological social worker's assessment of an older adult is not synonymous with what is often called a geriatric evaluation or diagnostic workup. *Geriatric evaluations* are usually done by a team of service providers, including physicians, social workers, psychologists, occupational therapists, speech pathologists, and physical therapists. Each professional evaluates an older adult within his or her own area of professional expertise, and then the team develops intervention and treatment plans. The term *diagnostic workup* most commonly refers to an in-depth medical or psychiatric evaluation of an older adult that is requested after presenting evidence of a medical or psychiatric problem. Although both geriatric evaluations and diagnostic workups are important parts of the continuum of care for older adults, they are ordinarily preceded by a more basic evaluation referred to in this chapter as a biopsychosocial assessment.

THE PURPOSE OF A BIOPSYCHOSOCIAL ASSESSMENT

An assessment serves as the basis for identifying how support or rehabilitative services can help older adults to maintain independent and satisfying lifestyles. An assessment also serves as an educational process to alert both the older adult and the appropriate support systems to high-risk areas that may threaten the older adult's well-being. Assessments are usually conducted following a change in the older adult's life, such as a serious illness, fall, loss of a spouse, change in living arrangements, or some evidence of difficulty observed by a family member or caregiver. An honest and thorough assessment should identify areas in which an older adult functions adequately as well as those in which an older adult faces significant challenges. Once strengths and challenges are identified, services can be specified that are aimed at supporting, restoring, or replacing levels of functioning.

Evaluation of Strengths and Challenges

It is deceptively easy to think of assessment as the process of evaluating what an older adult cannot do. Society tends to focus on what the body and the mind lose as the aging process occurs, rather than focusing on what capabilities are retained (or even improved) as people move into their later years. For example, older adults who have difficulty managing stairs may turn a downstairs room into a bedroom rather than take the risk of falling on the stairs. This process represents an older adult's attempt to "miniaturize" his or her environment, an effort to shrink personal space into a more manageable area (Rubenstein, Kilbride, & Nagy, 1992). Although it may appear to the social worker that the older adult can no longer live in a lifetime home, this move is actually an indication that the older adult has considered how to maintain control and mastery over a smaller environment, rather than consider moving out of familiar living space, a strength, not a weakness. Likewise, an older adult may spend most of the time in a single, comfortable chair surrounded by the phone, television, and important papers to minimize the number of times he or she has to get up and walk around, a functional adjustment to mobility and ambulation challenges. These are excellent examples of resilience and adaptability employed by older adults to cope with physical challenges creatively.

Applying a strengths perspective to both assessment and intervention means that every effort on the part of the social worker is focused on helping older adults to discover and employ their own strengths, mobilizing their capabilities, not deficits, to help them solve problems and achieve their own service goals (Chapin, Nelson-Becker, & MacMillan, 2006).

Identification of Ways to Support and Maintain Existing Functioning

The assessment process is helpful in identifying those areas in which older adults are functioning adequately but may benefit from additional support to maintain self-sufficiency. One of the most important underlying principles in gerontological social work is the merit of maximizing independent functioning and promoting maintenance of personal dignity for older adults. With this principle in mind, assessment should be focused, in part, on those areas in which older adults are maintaining independent functioning or are capable of doing so with some support. For example, an older widower may decide to give up driving because of steadily deteriorating eyesight. Although this is a wise decision from the perspective of safety to self and others, that choice has other consequences. It jeopardizes his daily attendance at the local senior center, where he gets his noon meal and plays cards with friends. To maintain and support his own initiatives to seek socialization outside his home, an assessment can appropriately identify that the older adult needs transportation, not necessarily the delivery of homebound meals. Delivering home meals may address the nutritional concern, but it deprives the older adult of his initiative in maintaining critical social contacts. Assessment can correctly identify ways in which to encourage and maintain an older adult's efforts to maximize independent functioning and meet personal needs.

Identification of Interventions and Supports That Restore Lost Functioning

Many of the therapeutic interventions discussed in this text address the importance of working to improve lost functioning. Using music or art therapy to help an older adult through a deep depression has the ultimate goal of alleviating the depression, not expecting that the older adult will simply learn to live with it. Physical and occupational therapy work specifically toward rehabilitating an older adult after an illness or accident to maximize abilities. Assessments can be helpful in identifying what functional capabilities have been compromised and what services might be provided to work toward reestablishing those abilities. For example, a recent widow who relied on her husband to drive her to shopping and medical appointments may need to learn to use public transportation to resume her independence in these areas. An older diabetic who has lost a foot to circulatory problems associated with the disease may have to learn to use a prosthetic device to regain mobility or make physical adaptations in his or her house to accommodate a wheelchair.

Complementing existing functioning with support services to replace lost functioning helps to reinforce an older adult's ability to maintain independence. For example, an older woman who has just suffered a minor stroke may be evaluated to determine if it is realistic for her to return to her own home. An assessment may determine that she can handle the basic activities of daily living, such as getting around her home, using the bathroom independently, and feeding herself, but she needs assistance in taking a bath several times a week or having meals delivered. An assessment can identify what functioning has been compromised as well as what independent functioning remains.

Sometimes the assessment process is crucial in helping families and support systems move beyond denial about an older adult's abilities to maintain independent living.

It is painful to see a loved one become frail, and it is easy to hide behind reluctance to seek more skilled assistance for the older adult, especially when the older adult resists added care. Data gathered from an assessment can provide an important basis for honest, although difficult, discussions between older adults and their families.

SPECIAL CONSIDERATIONS IN ASSESSING OLDER ADULTS

The Heterogeneity of the Older Adult Population

As has been reinforced throughout this text, the older adult population is very heterogeneous; therefore, social workers' approaches to the assessment process should be unique to each older adult. Most older adults are able to be very active participants in the assessment process with honest and forthcoming insights as to their own abilities as well as their needs. The purpose of an assessment is to help older adults get their needs met, not their needs as the social worker sees them. Other older adults may show more limited abilities to either participate in the process or recognize their own limitations. Severe hearing and sight losses may preclude using standard assessment tools or make verbal communication extremely difficult. For some older adults, the mere idea of being tested for basic competencies may produce such high levels of anxiety that they are unable or unwilling to participate. For yet others, the ravaging effects of dementia or depression preclude the older adult from even being emotionally or cognitively available to the assessor.

Use a more conversational tone to minimize the testing atmosphere and reduce performance anxiety. Give older adults time to become comfortable with you, and do the assessment at their pace, not yours. Avoid professional jargon that confuses or frightens older adults, and be prepared to explain why you are asking any of the assessment questions. Older adults have a right to know what you are looking for and why in the assessment process.

The Balance between Independence and Dependence

It makes sense that the older adult has the most to gain by recognizing his or her own limitations and accepting services that will enhance daily functioning. However, the deep-seated fear of losing independence and being forced to leave home, no matter how unfounded, often keeps older adults from either recognizing or admitting functional limitations. These fears and concerns are so powerful that older adults may go to great lengths to deny or hide problems they are having. Although it would seem easier to have older adults move to more accessible living arrangements, the significance of maintaining independence at all costs out of the fear associated with being forced into an institution is a powerful determinant in creating denial about functional abilities. When circumstances dictate an assessment by a social worker or health-care professional, older adults often fear what the consequences of identifying functional impairments will be. It is important for the person conducting the assessment to be cognizant of the presence and power of this fear. Intervening in the lives of older adults may represent a threat to an older adult's attempt to maintain the precarious balance between independence and dependence.

Origin of the Request for Assessment

When an individual or family voluntarily requests assistance from a social service agency under normal circumstances, the social worker can assume the clients are at least marginally self-motivated to obtain supportive services to improve the quality of their lives. They alone stand to benefit (or not benefit) from their active participation in the change effort. If an older adult has requested assistance in a specific area, such as housekeeping services, a chore service, or homebound meal delivery, the assessment process might be seen as part of a more comprehensive service delivery system that helps the older adult obtain not only the requested service but also others as they are deemed appropriate. In this situation, the request for assessment and intervention is client centered. The gerontological social worker can expect clients to be more directly involved in being active participants in the assessment process. It is a more straightforward process to work with older adults in identifying service needs when they have initiated contact with the service provider and can remain actively involved in the process of self-determination of any service plans. The older adult can remain in control of how little or how much intervention occurs.

However, in gerontological social work, a request for assessment and intervention is frequently not initiated by the older adult. The situation is much more complicated when an assessment has been requested by members of an older adult's family, other caregivers, neighbors, or even public service personnel, such as a police officer. The purpose and goals of an assessment under these circumstances are not as clear. It is important for the social worker to approach the assessment process with a clear understanding of whose goals are being addressed. Has the older adult consented to involvement with a social service agency, or is intervention by the social service community being initiated against the older adult's will? Is the older adult competent to make the decision to refuse intervention? What does the family or caregiver expect to be the result of the assessment process? Are these expectations consistent with the social work profession's commitment to self-determination? These are important questions to consider before the actual assessment process begins so that both the social worker and the older adult are clear about the stated purpose of the assessment.

Assessing and evaluating an older adult who actively opposes such intervention is similar to working with an involuntary client, and the social worker can anticipate considerable resistance. Children and adolescents may have little choice about receiving treatment due to a more restrictive perspective about their legal rights as minors. However, older adults retain full legal rights to self-determine, unless determined to be in need of guardianship under a strict legal procedure. The rights and wishes of the older adult's family or caregivers do not supersede the rights of the older adult.

Respecting Personal Privacy

One of the most important values of the social work profession is its commitment to respecting the personal dignity of the individual. In most social service settings, clients are asked to disclose some of the most personal aspects of their lives. The profession is often guilty of judging clients' receptiveness to intervention on the basis of how much of this personal information they are willing to discuss. If clients share this information willingly, they are considered cooperative. If they resist discussing highly personal information with a social worker they have just met, they too often are labeled resistant. Neither of these labels is accurate. The sphere of the deeply personal is one that is aggressively protected by most clients. For older adults who may never have come in contact with the social service delivery system, a social worker's attempt to obtain deeply personal information may be interpreted as rude, inappropriate, and intrusive. Assessments require that the social worker ask very personal questions about health, social relationships, and finances that may be particularly uncomfortable for older adults to answer. Although the social worker may understand the health risks involved with incontinence and know the condition can often be treated successfully, it is unrealistic to expect that older adults will be willing to share the details of their toileting habits. Admitting to a near stranger that one has lost control over urinary output may be intolerably embarrassing for an older adult. Similarly, the social worker may recognize that occasional memory lapses may be indicative of early dementia that may be treatable, but an older adult's fears of having Alzheimer's disease may understandably cause the older adult to deny such problems. The embarrassment of not knowing exactly what day it is or who is president of the United States may result in an older adult becoming resistant or belligerent as a legitimate defense mechanism. Perhaps the most sensitive area for older adults may be the area of financial resources. If a person has been socialized over his or her lifetime not to ask others about their finances and not to expect others to ask about personal finances, talking to a social worker about money may be extremely difficult. This holds true for older adults who have no money as well as those who have considerable resources.

CONDITIONS FOR CONDUCTING AN ASSESSMENT

The Physical Environment

The ideal place for an assessment to be done is the older adult's home. This places the older adult on his or her own turf, reducing the distractions and anxieties inevitable in an unfamiliar setting. The home setting also provides the social worker with invaluable information to corroborate or challenge what the older adult says about the ability to function. More details about what to look for in an older adult's home will be presented later in this chapter when the actual assessment process is discussed. When the assessment takes place in a hospital or other institutional setting, the social worker may not have much control over the setting. However, keeping the older adult in the room or space to which he or she has become accustomed is still more beneficial than moving to an unfamiliar location.

Some basic conditions in the physical setting can be controlled, regardless of a home or institutional setting. Make sure the older adult has access to any assistive devices, such as hearing aids, glasses, dentures, or mobility devices, such as a walker or cane. It is also crucial that there be adequate lighting in the setting so that the older adult can see any written materials being used and have a clear view of the social worker conducting the assessment. Minimize distractions caused by open doors, background noise, or annoying glare. Radios and televisions should be turned off to ensure that the older adult can hear and see the interviewer without interference.

If the assessment involves obtaining specific information on medications, medical record, or financial information, older adults should be given ample opportunity to locate the records in question prior to the assessment to have them available at the time of the interview. Older adults will be more confident during the interview if they have a basic understanding of what the assessment process entails.

Although family members, neighbors, and medical personnel may eventually be helpful in obtaining additional information for an assessment, try to conduct the first assessment session alone with the older adult. Having a spouse or family member present may influence the content of the answer and increase the likelihood that others will attempt to answer questions for the older adult.

Optimum Functioning

Select a time for the assessment when the older adult is not fatigued or feeling poorly. For older adults with serious health problems, fatigue may preclude their participation in a lengthy session of questions and answers. If the assessment is lengthy and detailed, schedule it over several shorter periods of time. Older adults with some organic brain damage may find mornings and late afternoons disorienting times of the day, making these poor times of the day to obtain an accurate picture of their functioning.

Be sensitive to cultural and gender issues that influence the quality of the interaction between the social worker and older adult. If English is not an older adult's first language, arrange for a skilled interpreter who is familiar with the assessment process, not just someone who happens to speak the language. Some Latina and Asian-American women may be extremely uncomfortable sharing deeply personal information with male social workers. Use family members to gauge what special arrangements need to be made.

Explaining the Purpose of the Assessment

It is not uncommon for family members to request an assessment of an older adult and then ask the social worker not to divulge that information to the older adult. Participating in such deceptive practices is unethical and ill advised. The older adult needs to know very specifically the purpose of the evaluation, who requested the assessment (if he or she did not), and for what end the findings will be used. The older adult must be able to consent to the assessment to engage him or her in the mutual process of identifying strengths and challenges. This process of securing informed consent is one of the most basic ethical principles of the social work profession.

In cases where older adults are not able to give their informed consent or appear unable to competently understand the purpose of the assessment, every effort should be made to protect their rights and dignity. Even if older adults do not appear to be able to fully understand the assessment process, social workers should take the time to explain it to them anyway. The explanatory process is a safeguard to the worker that he or she is clear about the purpose and is making a concerted effort to show professional respect for the older adult. Family members or designated caregivers need to be completely aware of the dynamics of the assessment process and who will have access to the findings when an older adult has limited cognitive abilities.

The Issue of Confidentiality

It is tempting for a social worker to assure a client that everything he or she says will remain absolutely confidential. In assessments of older adults, this is simply not true and should not be used as a way to encourage older adults to share personal information.

Other parties will see the findings of an assessment. Documentation of need is required to determine eligibility for many supportive and rehabilitative services to older adults. A visiting nurse will have access to pertinent medical information on the older adult. The Social Security Administration will see private financial information if an older adult applies for Supplemental Security Income. An art or music therapist will see the documentation of depression or dementia as part of planning intervention services. It is the social worker's responsibility to advise the older adult about what efforts are made to disclose this information only as is absolutely necessary to service providers and/or family members with a vested interest in the older adult's well-being. Older adults need to be reassured that personal information will be respected and protected within the confines of a specific circle of concerned parties. The obligation to explain honestly the parameters of confidentiality falls on the social worker.

COMPONENTS OF A COMPREHENSIVE ASSESSMENT

The specific aspect of an older adult's functioning that is assessed is determined by the purpose of the assessment. For an older adult who has no identified physical or medical problems but has shown evidence of serious depression, the social worker may only be evaluating the older adult's mental health. For an older adult who has shown no emotional or cognitive problems but struggles with the activities of daily living, a functional assessment of those abilities may be the focus of the assessment. The eight major domains included in a comprehensive assessment are physical health, competence in activities of daily living, psychological and emotional well-being, social functioning, spirituality, sexuality, financial resources, and environmental safety. The material included in these domains may be used in its entirety, or portions may be excerpted to focus on a specific area of concern. A standard form to be used for an assessment is not presented because most agencies and institutions have a specific format designed for their own purposes. Additional measurement tools social workers might find helpful to provide further validation to their own observations are presented when appropriate. This chapter is intended to give an overview of the general assessment process. The rest of the chapters in the book will go into more detail about specific issues in mental health and social relationships.

The most important activity the social worker can employ is a willingness to observe, to gather as much information as possible from those observations, and to engage the older adult continually in the assessment process as an active participant. Open your eyes and look. Open your ears and listen.

Getting Started on an Assessment

Basic Demographic Information

Obtaining basic demographic information first is helpful for several reasons. It is essential that an older adult's name, address, date of birth, and marital status are correctly recorded for future use. The process of gathering this information gives the older adult an opportunity to become more comfortable with the social worker and to prevent an older adult's immediate feeling of being "tested." To acquire a more personal picture of the older adult, it is helpful to find out about family members, including siblings and grandchildren, if any, to begin to identify potential support systems. Ask about employment status, military history, and education. Be prepared to listen to more details than you may need for the assessment. Older adults may use this opportunity to test your willingness to listen to them or to show their pride in their own or family members' accomplishments. It is worth the time it takes to help the older adult relax and feel comfortable with you.

Ask about a Typical Day

One approach that is helpful to starting off the assessment focusing as much on strengths as on challenges is to ask an older adult to describe a typical day for him or her. When does he or she get up? How does the older adult take care of essentials such as bathing or dressing? Is preparing breakfast part of his or her routine? Watching television? Reading the newspaper? Going online? Asking the older adult to describe what a typical day is like avoids the pressure of "test anxiety" and gives the social worker a valuable insight as to how the older adult views his or her own capabilities. Such an approach can feel more like a friendly visit than a more threatening assessment. Does the older adult have regularly scheduled activities outside the home or visits from friends or family members? What kinds of activities does the older adult engage in during the day if he or she rarely goes out of the home? What are highlights of the day? The part of the day that may be most difficult or lonely? What the older adult chooses to share with the social worker is incredibly valuable in terms of the older adult's perception of what he or she can still do despite limitations, the true essence of the strengths approach to working with older adults. The older adult will likely want to emphasize strengths as much as possible. The information shared during this part of the assessment also serves as a valuable segue into questions that come later in the assessment. For example, if an older adult mentions that he or she usually does not eat breakfast, later in the assessment when addressing functional abilities, it will seem less threatening to ask, "You mentioned that you usually do not eat breakfast. Is that because you have never been a breakfast eater or because it is difficult for you to cook breakfast?"

Physical Health

Physical Limitations

Using what you have learned about the normal changes associated with biological aging, carefully observe what physical changes are affecting the older adult. What is your first impression about the older adult's health? Does he or she have difficulty in walking, in getting up from sitting, or with physical coordination? Do you see evidence of tremors or paralysis? Is there any evidence of a prior stroke, such as slurred speech or weakness on one side of the body? Older adults who are having transient ischemic attacks (TIAs) display varying levels of awareness and may appear to be having brief "spells" of distraction or discomfort.

Is the older adult aware of any heart trouble? Is there any indication the older adult has trouble breathing or appears winded after simple activity? When asking older adults about hypertension, high blood pressure, some may use the term *high blood* to describe the condition. Likewise, older adults may refer to diabetes as *sugar*. If you do not understand the terms an older adult uses to describe a health condition, ask for clarification.

What prescription medication is the older adult taking, and what is it prescribed for? Also, it is critical to ask about OTC medications, which older adults may not even consider to be medications. Ask to see the bottles to confirm the accuracy of the description and to check for outdated medication. What assistive devices are needed, such as glasses, hearing aids, or mobility devices?

Although only a physician or nurse can professionally evaluate an older adult's health, it is important to obtain basic medical information from the older adult as part of the assessment process. What does the older adult identify as medical problems, past or present? Is she or he under a physician's regular care? Who is the physician or other health-care provider? Is the older adult receiving health care from other providers, such as a chiropractor, herbal healer, or acupuncturist?

Between one and two million older adults each year are the victims of physical, psychological, or other forms of abuse (National Center on Elder Abuse, 2005). Part of the physical assessment process includes looking for signs of older adult abuse. Does the older adult have suspicious bruises or signs of physical injury that she or he seems uncomfortable talking about? Does the older adult change his or her story about how an injury occurred during the course of the assessment? Older adults have more fragile skin than younger persons, so what is a minor injury for a younger person may appear as a more serious bruise for an older adult. If the older adult has a caregiver, try to ask about suspicious bruises and injuries when the caregiver is out of the room. If you suspect older adult abuse, contact the appropriate local office of Adult Protective Services through your local county department of social services immediately. The problem of the abuse and neglect of older adults and how to detect it is discussed in greater detail in Chapter 9.

Sensory Limitations

Is an older adult's hearing impaired? Older adults who have a hearing loss may nod and appear to hear you, but fail to answer questions appropriately or ignore your questions. The television may be turned up extremely loud, or the older adult may fail to answer the phone or a doorbell when it rings. Hearing loss makes communication tenuous. It is difficult to get accurate answers to assessment questions if you have serious concerns about whether the older adult has even heard you. Furthermore, older adults may be extremely self-conscious about hearing loss and deny it exists, making communication very frustrating. Figure 4.1 offers some helpful suggestions in how to communicate more effectively with older adults who have a hearing loss.

Figure 4.1 • Tips on Speaking to Older Adults with Hearing Loss

- Face the person and speak clearly.
- Stand where there is good lighting and low background noise.
- Speak slowly and distinctly.
- Do not put your hands over your mouth, eat, or chew gum.
- Use facial expressions or gestures to give useful clues.
- Reword your question if necessary.
- Be patient; stay positive and relaxed.
- Ask how you may help the listener to better understand you.
- If speaking in public, use a microphone.

Source: National Institute on Aging, (2002).

It is equally important in the process of assessment to determine whether an older adult has significant vision impairment. A person with sight loss may squint or tilt his or her head toward the speaker when spoken to, in an attempt to focus on the source of a voice, or may have difficulty locating personal objects in plain sight. When a vision-impaired older adult reaches out for objects, he or she may appear tentative, indicating an attempt to feel for an item rather than locate it with the eyes first and then reach for it. Some older adults have difficulty identifying color or may dress in inappropriate color combinations. Older adults who once found reading enjoyable may give up reading any materials because they cannot read anything that is not magnified significantly. Just watching an older adult moving across a room can give the social worker clues as to sight loss. An older adult may bump into the walls or objects in plain view or stumble on carpets, even though the surface is smooth. While eating, an older adult with vision loss may have difficulty getting food on a fork or serving himself or herself from a serving plate. Knocking over cups and glasses and having difficulty determining when a cup or glass is full are common problems for older adults with vision impairments (American Foundation for the Blind, 2007).

Self-Rating of Health

It is important to ask older adults how they rate their own health. Do they consider themselves healthy? What would they identify as any major health concerns? Do health problems prevent them from doing things they would like to do? Despite any health conditions, what activities have they been able to continue? Have other family members expressed concerns about their health? There are both objective and subjective components to self-rating of one's health status. Older adults with lifelong chronic illnesses may have adjusted well to their medical conditions and describe themselves as relatively healthy when you would not describe them as such. For example, an older woman with arthritis in her knees, cataracts, and poor hearing may say "but I can still work in my garden if I sit rather than kneel and given a partner (and my hearing aid), I could still dance!" She is focusing on what she can still do, not what she cannot. Give older adults the opportunity to brag about what they can do and how they adapt to issues in their own health.

Finally, after you have explored many of these areas with the older adult, is what the older adult tells you about his or her health consistent with what you have observed during the assessment? If an older adult claims no problems with hearing or sight, does that appear to be the case from your perspective? If an older adult denies any mobility limitations, does that coincide with what you observe? Assessment is a dynamic process in which the worker's observations and the older adult's insights both contribute to the final designation of problem areas. If your observations differ significantly from the older adult's responses, consider why this may be the case. Does the older adult appear to be afraid of having to leave his or her home? Are your expectations of adequate functioning unrealistic? If the older adult has not been receiving regular medical care, it may be helpful to advise him or her to have a physical exam and even to offer help make the appointment. Obtaining permission to review the results of any recent medical tests is essential to corroborating your and the older adult's assessment of physical health but should only be pursued if germane to future planning for services. Visiting nurses and home health-care aides traditionally do their own medical evaluations and are more professionally competent to interpret a physician's findings.

Competence in the Activities of Daily Living

Activities of Daily Living

An assessment of an older adult's physical well-being is a logical precursor to the discussion of functional assessment. Assessing an older adult's competence in the activities of daily living (ADLs) determines his or her ability to complete the basic tasks of self-care, such as eating, toileting, ambulating and transferring, bathing, dressing, and grooming. These functional abilities are influenced by the physical and psychological status of the older adult as he or she interfaces with the demands of everyday life. Major limitations in one or more of the ADLs strongly suggest an older adult needs supportive services unavailable in independent living without 24-hour care. Can an older adult feed himself or herself without assistance, or does he or she require assistance in cutting foods into bite-sized pieces or with buttering bread (eating)? Can an older adult get to toilet facilities at the appropriate time and control bodily elimination (toileting)? Is an older adult able to get around the living space (ambulation) and get out of bed or a chair without assistance (transfer)? Can an older adult bathe independently in a bathtub, in a shower, or by sponge bath? Is an older adult able to select clothing, dress independently, and accomplish basic grooming activities, such as combing hair or completing basic dental care?

Instrumental Activities of Daily Living

Instrumental activities of daily living (IADLs) are more complicated tasks than ADLs, yet remain basic skills necessary to managing an independent household, such as using a telephone or preparing meals. Losses in the ability to perform IADLs may signal the beginning of cognitive decline for older adults or the development of disabling health problems. Significant IADLs include the following:

1. Use of the telephone, including the ability to look up and dial a number and receive a call

2. Shopping, including the ability to plan and purchase items if transportation is provided

3. Food preparation, including both planning a complete meal and preparing it without assistance

4. Housekeeping skills, including heavy housework, such as scrubbing floors, or basic chores, such as dusting or making the bed

5. Independent transportation by car, bus, or taxi

6. Administration of medication, including taking the correct dosage at the appropriate time without assistance or reminder from others

7. Money management, including writing checks or securing money orders to pay bills

These activities are usually evaluated on one of three levels: retains the ability to accomplish the activity completely independently, needs assistance in some part of the activity, or is unable to do the task at all. Impairments in any of the IADLs do not necessarily imply an older adult is unable to live independently; rather, they suggest support services may be needed to help maintain as much independence as possible. A credible functional assessment requires a combination of both an older adult's response to the questions posed and the social worker's own direct observations. What evidence do you have to support or refute the older adult's assessment of his or her functioning in each of the areas? It is painful for older adults to admit to others they have difficulties performing activities of daily living that they successfully accomplished throughout their adult lives.

Psychological Functioning

Compiling an accurate picture of an older adult's psychological functioning begins at the moment you begin interacting with him or her. While talking to the older adult about physical health and functional abilities, you will begin to get a preliminary idea of how he or she is able to process and answer questions, recall factual information, and carry on a logical and coherent conversation. Included in psychological functioning for the purpose of an assessment are personality, intelligence, memory, dementia, and delirium.

Personality

Personality is part of a person's psychological functioning and provides insight into how a person views the world and copes with stress. How would you describe the older adult's personality? Ask how he or she has changed since being younger. What are areas of the older adult's life that he or she considers to be great sources of stress? If an older adult mentions a particularly stressful event, such as a serious illness or death of a friend or family member, explore how he or she has coped with the stress. What accomplishments is the older adult proud of? What have been the greatest joys in his or her life? These questions will help you get at the self-perceived strengths of the older adult. The answers will also give you insight as to how well the older adult is able to mobilize problem-solving skills. Do you get the sense the older adult feels control over his or her life or simply reacts as events happen? An older adult's sense of mastery over his or her life is one of the strongest predictors of emotional well-being (Rubenstein, Kilbride, & Nagy, 1992).

Intelligence

What is your basic evaluation of the older adult's intelligence? How does the older adult keep mentally active—by reading, solving crossword puzzles, or other intellectually stimulating activities? Educational level is not the most accurate indicator of an older adult's intellectual abilities, but rather how well he or she uses intellectual resources to problem solve or remain connected to life. Minimally educated older adults may be wonderfully creative and resourceful in maintaining a sense of mastery over their environment.

Memory

An older adult's personal assessment of his or her own memory is important to understanding any deterioration in memory functions. Does the older adult have more difficulty remembering recent or remote events? Do you notice a deliberate effort on the older adult's part to remember information, or does "I do not remember" come as a more automatic response? Does the older adult repeat certain pieces of information throughout the assessment without being aware of doing so? Try to determine whether the older adult is concerned about memory loss, unaware of it, or just accepts it as part of the aging process. Is what the older adult does not remember even important? An older adult may not remember what he or she had for lunch yesterday but can tell you every phone conversation he or she has had in the last week. Realistically, which is more important?

Dementia

Dementia is a gradual deterioration in an older adult's ability to process and express logical ideas, orient self to time and location, and access recent and remote memory. The most familiar kind of dementia among older adults is Alzheimer's disease, which is discussed in detail in Chapter 5. The purpose of a psychological assessment is not for the social work practitioner to diagnose dementia per se, but rather to document symptoms that suggest further testing for cognitive impairment is advisable. Dementia is caused by actual biological changes in the brain, and its onset is usually gradual rather than sudden. Although older adults suffering from dementia appear to have normal sleep patterns, appetite, and energy levels, they present with a sense of disorientation or confusion about common activities of daily living. They may exhibit a great deal of difficulty with basic intellectual activities, such as remembering the names of common objects, orienting themselves to the correct day of the month or season of the year, or counting. They may have difficulty concentrating or making simple decisions. The deficits appear in cognitive or intellectual functioning, not in severe alterations in mood or affect. An older adult may or may not be aware of these cognitive deficits, yet it is common for an older adult with some degree of dementia to confabulate, or make up an answer to a question, rather than respond, "I do not know." This is a conscious or unconscious attempt to minimize the loss of cognitive functioning.

A simple and commonly used tool used to identify dementia is the Mini-Mental Status Exam, examples of which appear in Figure 4.2 (Folstein, Folstein, & McHugh, 1975). The exam is intended to help the assessor determine if there are indications of cognitive limitations. An older adult is asked about orientation to time and space as well as tested for basic cognitive functions, such as using short-term memory, naming familiar objects, reading and following simple directions, and reproducing a simple line figure. The exam takes about 10 minutes to administer. Results of the exam can give the social worker a

Figure 4.2 • Sample Items from the Folstein Mini-Mental Status Exam (MMSE)

1. Orientation to Time
   "What is the date?"

2. Registration
   "Listen carefully, I am going to say three words. You say them back after I stop. Ready? Here they are . . .
   APPLE (pause), PENNY (pause), TABLE (pause). Now repeat those words back to me."
   (Repeat up to five times, but score only the first trial.)

3. Naming "What is this?"
   (Point to a pencil or pen.)

4. Reading "Please read this and do what it says."
   (Show examinee the words on the stimulus form.) CLOSE YOUR EYES.

baseline idea about the presence or absence of cognitive deficits, which may be indicative of dementia. This exam is not a definitive indicator of dementia but simply gives the assessor some preliminary indications of an older adult's cognitive functioning at the time of the assessment. If an older adult scores poorly on this test, more in-depth testing for cognitive limitations is advised.

Delirium

Unlike dementia, delirium is an acute, temporary condition that often mimics dementia. Delirium is characterized by disorientation, confusion, difficulty in making decisions, and decreased alertness, many of which are also symptoms of dementia. The primary difference is that the onset of delirium is rapid and usually connected to an identifiable, precipitating event, such as a toxic reaction to medications, dehydration, poor nutrition, an infection, acute alcohol withdrawal, or hypothermia (American Psychiatric Association, 2000). Older adults suffering from delirium may have fluctuating levels of awareness and present with disorganized thinking and severely impaired memory. Both emotional and intellectual stability appear to be impaired with this condition, and the older adult may experience hallucinations or delusions. Families usually notice the sudden change in functioning following an illness or other event in the older adult's life. Delirium is a medical emergency and warrants immediate medical treatment to minimize permanent damage. It is not constructive or medically advised to try to conduct an assessment of an older adult who shows symptoms of delirium. Delirium is discussed in greater detail in Chapter 5.

Emotional Well-Being

Depression

Assessing emotional well-being in the older adult requires determining whether the older adult's emotional state is stable and appropriate. For example, does the older adult appear to be depressed or verbally indicate that he or she feels sad or listless much of the time? Everyone has days when they feel blue or sad, but a prolonged state of sadness is not a normal part of the aging process. Find out if the older adult has suffered a recent loss, such as the death of a spouse, family member, or close friend. In these situations, some level of depression is expected and should not be considered problematic unless the depressed state persists for an extremely long time. The two primary characteristics of a serious depression are a depressed mood and a markedly diminished interest in activities that were a source of pleasure for the older adult (American Psychiatric Association, 2000). Secondary characteristics include an extreme feeling of sadness, frequent crying spells, and disruptions in normal sleep patterns, which may include either insomnia or excessive sleeping. Depressed persons usually voice a feeling of chronic fatigue and a loss of normal levels of energy. Older adults may focus on what they can no longer do rather than on what strengths and abilities have not been impaired by illness or the general process of aging. Rather than confabulating, as is more apparent in persons with dementia, depressed persons may answer many questions with the response "I do not know," showing little, if any, effort to think about the answer to the question. Depressed older adults often have great difficulty making even the simplest decisions, such as what to eat or what to do in a familiar situation. In interviewing a depressed older adult, one often gets the sense that he or she simply no longer cares about much in life or cannot rally the energy to participate in any activities (Mosher-Ashley & Barrett, 1997). A more in-depth discussion of the clinical indicators of serious depression appears in Chapter 5.

Suicidal Ideation

A depressed older adult may express feelings of personal worthlessness and have recurring thoughts of death or suicidal ideation. Suicide is the 10th leading cause of death among persons over the age of 65 (Center for Disease Control, 2005). The risk for suicide among older adults is 50 percent greater than among younger populations (Kissane & McLaren, 2006). At particular risk for suicide are older adults who have experienced a recent change in living situations, such as being widowed or moving from a lifetime home or apartment. White men in poor health who live alone, have a low socioeconomic status, and have few social supports are at particularly high risk.

An older adult's risk for suicide must be seriously considered in doing any assessment of emotional well-being. A number of simple questions should be asked during the process of an assessment to clearly determine whether an older adult is at increased suicide risk and should be immediately referred for psychiatric evaluation. They include the following:

- Have you ever felt life was not worth living? If yes, when?
- Have you ever considered ending your life? If yes, when?
- Do you feel that way now?
- Have you ever considered how you would do it?
- Do you have a plan?
- What has stopped you from going through with your plan?

These questions should be included in every gerontological assessment, even if you do not consider the older adult depressed on the basis of your observations of his or her mood and affect. A more comprehensive look at suicide among older adults is included in Chapter 8. The threat to commit suicide should never be discounted or minimized. Take immediate action if an older adult appears to be at high risk.

Anxiety and Worry

Whereas depression is characterized by a long-standing sense of sadness and hopelessness, anxiety is defined as a sense of chronic internal discomfort, dread, a deep foreboding that something bad is going to happen, accompanied by physical symptoms of hyperventilation, nervousness, headache, or trembling (Mohlman et al., 2004). Older adults may seem to be easily distracted or deeply worried about events that may or may not happen. It may be difficult for them to concentrate on simple tasks; attempts to recall factual information may be impaired by their agitated state. Medical conditions—such as cardiovascular problems, Parkinson's disease, Alzheimer's disease, and hormonal imbalances—often mimic the symptoms of anxiety and should be considered before describing an older adult as suffering from anxiety. Anxiety is also easily confused with worry. Worry is related to specific concerns about identifiable issues, and the older adult is usually able to discuss exactly what he or she is worrying about (Diefenbach et al., 2003). Worry itself is not a pathological response but a legitimate emotional reaction to health and safety concerns. It is important to probe an older adult's concerns when conducting an assessment to make this important distinction.

Social Functioning

The purpose of assessing social functioning is to determine what, if any, social activities an older adult participates in or would like to participate in and to determine whether an older adult has social supports he or she feels can be mobilized.

Lifestyle

The older adult's description of a typical day in his or her life discussed earlier in this chapter is the basis for learning about how an older adult views his or her own life. The description may help you discern what kind of worldview the older adult has constructed. This is the core of the social constructionist understanding of the social process of aging. Activity, disengagement, and continuity theories of social aging posit that older adults have unique ways of retaining and discarding activity patterns from earlier in their lives. Does the older adult remain engaged in the mainstream of life, or has he or she withdrawn from a more active life? Have any life events forced the older adult to unwillingly adopt a less-active life? If so, has the older adult made an attempt to substitute different activities for those lost?

Social Isolation

Does the older adult feel lonely and want more social interaction with others? How often does an older adult leave home to visit friends or family, attend religious services, or other social activities, such as senior center gatherings, religious activities, a card club, shopping, or attending concerts? What transportation is available to the older adult? Would the older adult like to leave home more often? If the answer is yes, what obstacles prevent the older adult from doing so? Not every older adult wants to be busy socializing all the time. Respect the older adult's wish to spend time alone. There is no specific right or wrong answer to any of these questions, but problem areas can be identified if the older adult is not happy with the current situation and sincerely wants to have more social contact. Some older adults are extremely content spending lots of time alone and would never describe themselves as lonely.

Vanderhorst and McLaren (2005) found that fewer social supports are correlated with higher levels of depression and suicidal ideation. It is important for the social worker to recognize and acknowledge the significance of losses in an older adult's life. Social roles—such as spouse, worker, community member, or friend—may be lost in old age and never replaced. These losses seriously affect the number and quality of social interactions for the older adult.

Lubben and Gironda (2003) have developed a short, six-question instrument, the Lubben Social Network Scale (LSNS-6), to assess support available from family members separately from that provided by friends and neighbors. This instrument is shown in Figure 4.3. Simply seeing family members does not guarantee social support from them, as an older adult may not feel comfortable sharing private matters or feel at ease asking for specific kinds of assistance. The same is true for friends and neighbors. Yet friends and neighbors may provide the most important kind of support, regular social contact not obligated by family ties. This instrument assists the social worker in identifying both the strengths and challenges of the older adult's social support network.

Instrumental and Emotional Support

Instrumental support refers to any outside assistance the older adult may receive, such as financial support, help with household chores, or running errands. Ask the older adult who, if anyone, helps him or her in these areas. Is this arrangement satisfactory for both the older adult and the person providing instrumental support? Are there things the older adult cannot do because he or she cannot find someone to help? Answers to these questions will help you understand what support systems exist for the older adult and

Figure 4.3 • Lubben Social Network Scale-6

1. How many of your *relatives* do you see or hear from at least once a month?
2. How many of your *relatives* do you feel at ease with that you can talk about private matters?
3. How many *relatives* do you feel close to that you can call on them for help?
4. How many of your *friends* do you see or hear from at least once a month?
5. How many *friends* do you feel at ease with that you can talk about private matters?
6. How many *friends* do you feel close to that you can call on them for help?

Separate numerical subscales can be computed for the older adult's response to the "relatives" and "friends" questions or both can be combined to form a composite LSNS-6 score that can be used as a measure of social isolation (Lubben, 2006).

Source: Reprinted with permission from Oxford University Press.

what systems need to be developed. Gaps in instrumental support can often be closed by providing home-based services, such as homemaking or chore services, if family or friends are not available to help.

Emotional support is more personal and involves contact and support from family members or close friends. Who does the older adult contact when a problem arises or when he or she feels the need to talk to someone? Does he or she have a confidant with whom troubling or disturbing thoughts can be shared? Women tend to fare better in this area than men, primarily because women are more likely to develop and maintain a network of social relationships. The presence of even one close emotional friend can help an older adult ease the pain of loneliness and continue to feel connected to others.

Spirituality

An older adult's spirituality can be an important source of support as he or she faces the biopsychosocial challenges associated with the aging process. A healthy sense of one's spirituality has been associated with better mental health, an enhanced ability to cope with life events, and improved self-esteem (Nelson-Becker, Nakashima, & Canda, 2006). The role of spirituality in social work with older adults, including specific instruments for helping older adults identify its role in his or her life, is discussed in detail in Chapter 10, but it will be presented here as an essential part of the assessment process. Spirituality does not refer specifically to one's religious affiliation, although that may be part of how an older adult defines his or her spirituality. The concept of spirituality is intended to include transcendence beyond one's self, a search for meaning, and a sense of connectedness to others.

A brief assessment of an older adult's spirituality often begins with the older adult identifying his or her faith tradition or religion, if any. Is this the same faith tradition the older adult was raised in or has he or she changed affiliation as an adult? What level of involvement does the older adult have with a religious institution such as a church, synagogue, or mosque? What role does the older adult see this institution having in supporting him or her in life today? How important is this religious affiliation to the older adult?

Even if older adults do not identify a religious affiliation, their personal spirituality may be an important source of support. Dudley, Smith, and Millison (1995) suggested the following questions, which do not use specific religious language, as ways to discuss a person's spirituality: How does the person describe his or her philosophy of life? How does the person express his or her spirituality? What helps the person the most when he or she is afraid or needs special help? What does the person describe as being meaningful in his or her life at this time? What gives a person hope? These questions are just examples of how to help an older adult identify the role spirituality plays in his or her life and how spirituality might serve as a resource in assessing an older adult's strengths (or challenges) and in designing interventions (Nelson-Becker, Nakashima, & Canda, 2006).

Sexual Functioning

As discussed in Chapter 3, sexuality and sexual activity may or may not be important to an older adult. In the case of an acute health-care crisis, such as advanced dementia, a serious stroke, or physical illness, it may be inappropriate to ask an older adult about his or her interest in and concerns about sexuality until the crisis passes (Robinson & Molzahn, 2007). However, it is not inappropriate to discuss sexuality with an older adult when the crisis has passed, as it is often a concern of the older adult about how his or her illness will affect the ability to be sexually active. The physical or mental health-care provider should begin with a sensitive exploration of the issue, using a normative statement followed by a nonthreatening question, such as, "Despite health problems, many older adults continue to be sexually active. Is this important to you?" If an older adult reacts negatively to the question or responds with a statement about having been a widow or widower for a long time, the worker might assume sexuality or sexual activity is not an issue or the older adult has made a deliberate decision not to discuss the issue with the worker. If an older adult responds positively to such a question, a number of other follow-up questions will help the worker assess this area of psychosocial functioning. Wallace, Boltz, and Greenberg (2007) suggest asking older adults about how they express themselves sexually, if they have questions or concerns about fulfilling their sexual needs, how the sexual relationship with a spouse or partner has changed over time, and what the health-care provider can do to provide information or services that will help the older adults fulfill their sexual needs. These questions are not exhaustive but do give the worker a place to begin the discussion of sexuality with the older adult and to identify if there are ways in which meeting sexual needs can be incorporated into a service plan for the older adult. The social worker should never see himself or herself as an expert in this area without advanced training but may be helpful in answering an older adult's questions about sexual performance issues associated with the physical changes of aging, or access to medical interventions such as hormonal therapy or medication.

Financial Resources

If appropriate to the purpose of the assessment, ask an older adult about his or her financial resources. Although personal finances are a very sensitive topic with older adults, the topic can be broached by indirect questions. Does the older adult worry about having enough money for regular living expenses? Has he or she delayed getting a prescription filled or buying food because the money was not available? Is money available for emergency expenses? Exploring an older adult's financial resources may help identify other sources of financial or material assistance for which the older adult is eligible, such as Supplemental Security Income, Medical Assistance, or energy assistance. If an older adult believes that your questions are in his or her best interest in helping improve the quality of life, answers to questions about money may be more forthcoming. It is important to respect an older adult's personal privacy in this area.

Environmental Issues

Assessing the older adult's environment includes observations about the general repair of his or her home or apartment and the existence of a hazard-free living space. This is of specific concern for older adults in preventing injury from falls.

General Repair

Does the older adult's home or apartment appear to be properly maintained? Are basic housekeeping tasks attended to, such as keeping floors and windows clean, removing trash, and washing dishes? Does the older adult voice any concerns about these household chores?

How has the older adult decorated the home? Are there recent pictures of family and friends on display? Are clocks and calendars evident in the home, and are they set to the correct time and date? Most older adults take great pride in their homes, no matter how humble, and the home serves as much more than just a place to live. Rather, it is the stage on which they are living out their lives. Some older adults are financially and physically able to update home furnishings regularly, whereas others are more comfortable with old, familiar surroundings.

Hazard-Free Living Space

Older adults are at greater risk for falls due to age-related changes in sight, hearing, and coordination. Check the living space for furniture, rugs, or clutter in walkways that could cause an older adult to trip and fall. A checklist identifying specific questions about possible hazardous conditions appears in Figure 4.4. Look for drapery and electrical cords that are difficult to see and easy to stumble over. Do stairs have handrails? Is the home or apartment equipped with smoke and carbon monoxide detectors? Does the older adult have an emergency alert device that connects with the local police, fire department, or local hospital if assistance is needed? Are papers, magazines, or books piled up in a way that could be a fire hazard? Does the older adult appear to "hoard" items such as trash, food, or pets? The problem of hoarding among older adults is discussed in detail in Chapter 5.

Security Precautions

Many older adults have lived in the same location for many years while the neighborhood around them has changed significantly. How safe does the neighborhood appear to you? Are other people on the streets, or does the area appear abandoned? Does the older adult feel safe in the home? Although the socioeconomic class of the neighborhood is not always an issue for older adults, knowing how the older adult feels about leaving the home is an important consideration for future planning of activities. Does he or she have adequate locks on doors and windows? Too few? Too many? An excessive number of locks may indicate an older adult has had difficulty in the past or anticipates trouble with intruders in the future.

Figure 4.4 • Older Consumer Home Safety Checklist

Use this checklist to spot possible safety problems that may be present in the older adult's home. Check YES or NO to answer each of these questions. Then go back over the list and take action to correct those items that may need attention.

1. Are lamp, extension, and telephone cords placed out of the flow of traffic?	Yes	No
2. Are electrical cords in good condition, not frayed or cracked?	Yes	No
3. Do extension cords carry more than their proper load?	Yes	No
4. Are small rugs and runners slip-resistant?	Yes	No
5. Are emergency numbers posted on or near the telephone?	Yes	No
6. Are smoke detectors properly located?	Yes	No
7. Are smoke detectors working?	Yes	No
8. Are space heaters placed where they cannot be knocked over?	Yes	No
9. Are gas or kerosene heaters properly ventilated?	Yes	No
10. Does the older adult have an emergency exit plan? An alternative exit in case of fire?	Yes	No
11. Are hallways, passageways, between rooms and other heavy traffic areas well lit?	Yes	No
12. Are exits and passageways kept clear?	Yes	No
13. Are bathtubs and showers equipped with nonskid materials?	Yes	No
14. Are medications stored in the containers that they came in and are they clearly marked?	Yes	No
15. Are stairs equipped with handrails?	Yes	No
16. Is the lighting in the stairwells sufficient to prevent falls?	Yes	No

Source: Adapted from the U.S. Consumer Product Safety Commission (2011).

Professional Intuition

Finally, what are your general impressions about the older adult's ability to participate in the assessment process? How did the assessment "feel" to you? Are there items not included in any of the preceding sections of this chapter that alarmed you? What does your professional intuition tell you about the older adult's functioning? Trusting your professional intuition is an essential part of the assessment process and plays an important role in determining what areas you feel are particularly important to study further. If you do not feel you were able to get enough information from an older adult, it may be necessary to contact other collaterals to help you draw a solid conclusion about an older adult's functioning.

Using Collaterals to Gather Additional Information

If an older adult has serious cognitive or communicative difficulties, it may be necessary to involve other collaterals, such as family, friends, or other service providers, in the assessment process. It is important that the older adult give permission for you to contact other people and is aware that you will be asking for specific information about his or her abilities in all the areas of the assessment process. If family members are in regular contact with the older adult, they can be helpful in determining what difficulties in functioning have been present for a long time and which are most recent. How has the older adult changed in the past six months or in the past year? Was there a precipitating event, such as an illness or personal loss that exacerbated the problem? What has the family member noticed, if anything, about changes in mood, cognitive abilities, or social involvement? Be aware that families have lifelong, unresolved familial issues and be sensitive to personal agendas that may skew the accuracy of responses. Whatever goals are set for intervention will have an effect on family members as well. Other collaterals, such as lifelong friends, physicians, clergy, or even the postal carrier, may have insights that can help the social worker clarify both the strengths and challenges older adults face in their daily lives.

EXAMPLE OF A COMPREHENSIVE ASSESSMENT

Doing a comprehensive assessment involves obtaining what seems like a tremendous amount of information, but this material can be organized in a concise presentation that can be very useful not only to the social worker but to other physical or mental health-care professionals who work with the older adult. The key to writing up a meaningful assessment is to report the information in an organized, factual manner, highlighting both strengths and challenges that identify areas for intervention. The assessment narrative of Mrs. Alice Kingson covers all the areas included in a comprehensive biopsychosocial assessment. Read the material carefully thinking about what her strengths and challenges appear to be.

Mrs. Alice Kingson is a 76-year-old African-American woman who lives with her husband of 55 years, Charles, in their home, a modest bungalow. She was referred to Elder Services, with her permission, by the hospital discharge planner following her hospital-ization at Memorial Hospital for a stroke. The mild stroke left her with a pronounced weakness on her right side and some speech deficits. Although her husband is currently providing personal care and preparing all meals for Mrs. Kingson, this is not a long-term solution. Mr. Kingson has his own health problems and is simply overwhelmed by the demands of his wife's care.

Mrs. Kingson has four grown children, all of whom live within five miles of her. She has seven grandchildren and two great-grandchildren that she used to see almost every Sunday when they came for dinner at the Kingson home. Mrs. Kingson stayed home to raise her children until the youngest child was in school; she then returned to full-time work as a children's librarian. She continued working until 10 years ago, when she retired along with her husband. She was volunteering two days a week at a local school until she became ill.

Physical Health

Mrs. Kingson is a petite, attractive older woman who looks much younger than her age. When she is sitting down, it is difficult to see the physical damage from the stroke. She is able to walk, although she appears unsteady on her feet and drags her right leg. Her face droops on the right side from the stroke, but she has lively eyes and an easy smile. Her speech is slurred, but if she speaks slowly and methodically, she can easily be understood. Although Mrs. Kingson has always been under a physician's care for high blood pressure, she considered her health quite good until her recent "episode," as she describes her stroke. She is under regular medical care by an internist. She has arthritis in her hands and shoulders but claims that this has never interfered with her ability to take care of her grandchildren, do her housework, or be as active as she wants to be. Mrs. Kingson has a minor hearing loss for which she does not have (nor wants) a hearing aid. She wears glasses for reading and close work but has not had any problems with glaucoma or cataracts. She has no attention deficits and is able to answer all questions if she has a little more time to get her words out. Considering her speech limitations, she is very articulate. She is appropriately dressed but is wearing a sweater despite the warmth of the home.

Prior to her stroke, Mrs. Kingson was on Atenylol to control her high blood pressure but is now on medication to lower her cholesterol (Lipitor) and a low dose of Paxil to treat what she calls "her nerves." She receives the medications in a "blister pack" that shows her what medications should be taken at what time of the day. She clearly knows what each of the medications is for and when it should be taken. Mr. Kingson prepares both breakfast and lunch for the couple. Their daughter has been bringing the couple dinner every night. Mrs. Kingson appears adequately nourished. There are no apparent signs of either abuse or neglect.

Competence in the Activities of Daily Living

Mrs. Kingson's greatest limitations are apparent in her functioning in the activities of daily living, as she needs some assistance in bathing, dressing, and ambulation. She hates having to be dependent on her husband but she simply does not have the strength on her right side to do these things without help. She is able to use the phone and take her medication independently but is unable to prepare meals, do any housework, or transport herself independently. Mrs. Kingson's assessment of her own abilities seems to be consistent with the worker's observations. This appears to be the area where she will need the greatest amount of assistance.

Psychological Health

Mrs. Kingson is a delightful woman with an engaging personality and a good sense of humor, despite the damage from the stroke. Her reaction to her stroke was mainly one of confusion. She was feeling good, walking for about half an hour every day with her husband, and taking her medication regularly. She has difficulty understanding how this could happen to her and is eager for things to "get back to normal around here" as soon as possible. Even while being interviewed, Mrs. Kingson was flexing her right hand with a rubber ball to improve manual strength, as suggested by her physical therapist in the hospital.

Once an avid reader, Mrs. Kingson has problems reading now because holding a book is difficult, and her eyesight has been slightly affected by the stroke. Her physician feels the sight will return to normal after the swelling from the stroke has completely subsided, so she is hopeful she will be able to return to reading. She is getting very bored